Improving Staff Effectiveness in Human Service Settings

Organizational Behavior Management Approaches

Improving Staff Effectiveness in Human Service Settings

Organizational Behavior Management Approaches

Lee W. Frederiksen and Anne W. Riley
Editors

The Haworth Press
New York

Improving Staff Effectiveness in Human Service Settings: Organizational Behavior Management Approaches has also been published as *Journal of Organizational Behavior Management*, Volume 5, Numbers 3/4, Fall/Winter 1983.

The Haworth Press, Inc., 28 East 22 Street, New York, NY 10010

Library of Congress Cataloging in Publication Data
Main entry under title:

Improving staff effectiveness in human service settings.

    "Has also been published as Journal of organizational behavior management, v. 5, no. 3/4, fall/winter 1983."—T.p. verso.
    Includes bibliographical references and index.
    1. Social work administration—Addresses, essays, lectures. 2. Organizational behavior—Addresses, essays, lectures. I. Frederiksen, Lee W. II. Riley, Anne W.
HV41.I427   1984   361.3'068'3   84-722
ISBN 0-86656-282-6

Improving Staff Effectiveness in Human Service Settings

Organizational Behavior Management Approaches

Journal of Organizational Behavior Management
Volume 5, Numbers 3/4

CONTENTS

Section III: APPLICATIONS

Introduction

In many ways this volume is a response to the clamor about our problem-ridden human service system. It seems human services have become a favorite scapegoat for bureaucrats and citizens alike. But this need not be the case. This volume is a testimony that managers and administrators are innovatively and successfully making their agencies effective.

This special issue is also a demonstration. It demonstrates the effectiveness and the potential of Organizational Behavior Management in addressing the very real problems facing human service delivery. All of the interventions take place in actual human service settings. Several of these were encountering problems so severe that the existence of the facility was threatened. The reports reflect the potential of OBM for identifying, tracking, targeting and evaluating problems. But OBM is more than a collection of intervention techniques. It is also a theoretical framework that can direct the overall management of an organization.

In the first section the article by Anne Riley and Lee Frederiksen, "Organizational Behavior Management in Human Service Settings: Problems and Prospects," sets the stage for the following contributions by defining the multiple purposes and problems of human services. You will recognize such problems as the input/output problem, the organizational purpose problem, and the idealistic staff problem, though you may know them by other names. OBM is defined in a manner that contrasts and compares it with more traditional management approaches. Several specific applications and challenges arise from the integration of OBM into the management of the human services. These are considered along with directions for the future.

The second section of this volume is entitled *Developing Approaches to Effectiveness*. The articles in this section report interventions in applied settings. However, these interventions are more than program reports, they were designed to clarify and assess the effects of specific techniques and strategies in controlled studies.

In the first article, John Elder and his associates applied OBM to the development of a workable Quality Assurance program in a Community Mental Health Center. In a potential model for managers, they translate the goals of the program in a manner that provided realistic direction to staff. By focusing on one dimension of the Quality Assurance concept, they were able to change relevant staff behavior as well as to evaluate the impact of this change on client outcome measures.

The contribution by Johnson and Frederiksen also addresses the dual outcome issues of staff behavior and client response. In a multiple baseline design, staff treatment behavior increased dramatically when goal setting and feedback were employed. The assumption in this health care setting was that the targeted staff activity was therapeutically beneficial to the patient although that assumption had not been tested within this particular setting. By concomitantly evaluating staff activity and client response, these investigators clarified the relationship between this particular staff behavior and client response. The results did not support the assumptions. These authors discuss the importance and implications of such dual level investigations in our efforts to establish truly effective services.

The study by John Ford addresses one of the most pervasive and costliest issues managers face, staff training. This study employed a group design to compare a Personalized System of Instruction with the training program historically employed in the institution. It evaluated not only the effectiveness and efficiency of the two methods, but also the relative costs of training. The results have implications for the delivery of cost effective training in virtually all human service settings.

Section III, *Applications*, focuses on the application of OBM to a range of human service settings from high schools to day care centers to hospitals. The first of these is a "Description and Evaluation of an Approach to Implementing Programs in Organizational Settings" by Charles Maher. A seasoned investigator in the field, Dr. Maher has developed a comprehensive approach to program implementation. He provides two data based comparative evaluations of this strategy in action.

The following article, "A Case Study in the Programming and Maintenance of Institutional Change" by Pete Christian is perhaps the most comprehensive application of the principles and techniques of OBM to human service management. The author systematically identified and targeted the multiple problems threatening this institution for the developmentally disabled with loss of accreditation. He reports a well documented 5 year intervention that was successful in establishing this institution as an effective, respected and well-funded organization. The next case study also reports a large scale investigation. Craig Jensen and his colleagues document the impact of a series of upper management policy changes in a large institution for the developmentally disabled. Employing an innovative retrospective methodology, they document the effects and side effects of policy change on relevant staff and client measures.

The final contribution, ''A Case Study Examining the Effectiveness and Cost of Incentive Programs to Reduce Staff Absenteeism in a Preschool'' by Jinger Robins and Margaret Lloyd reports a 4 year evaluation. In a setting where even moderate levels of absenteeism threatened the ability of the organization to meet licensing requirements, these authors demonstrate cost effective incentive strategies that reduce absenteeism over a sustained period of time. Additionally, this study compared the relative effectiveness of two incentive programs.

In sum, these papers represent good news for the future of human services. There are clearly creative people committed to the implementation of well evaluated cost effective staff management strategies. Transforming human services into the effective, accountable agencies demanded by those from within and without the system will progress slowly. Change, especially effective change, takes time. But the impetus is strong and as this volume reflects, the strategy and models are available.

Lee W. Frederiksen
Anne W. Riley

Improving Staff Effectiveness in Human Service Settings

Organizational Behavior Management Approaches

Section I:

A PERSPECTIVE

Organizational Behavior Management in Human Service Settings: Problems and Prospects

Anne W. Riley
Lee W. Frederiksen

The vast human service system in this country undoubtedly provides services to virtually all Americans at sometime in their lives. While these services are typically taken for granted on an individual level, they are often vociferously attacked on an institutional and policy level. Regrettably, the concern that these agencies have become inadequate to their tasks do have a basis. The frequently cited problems of inefficient use of resources, drastically increasing costs which burden taxpayers and lack of demonstrably effective interventions make it difficult to substantially refute these concerns.

Yet despite the sometimes justified criticism it is unlikely that the human services will cease to exist. They serve many critical functions in modern day society. They serve needs that would be difficult or impossible to meet without radical alterations in the very fabric of developed society. The question then becomes, "Can they be made more effective?" It is our contention that they can be. More specifically, we assert that Organizational Behavioral Management (OBM) can serve a significant role in improving the effectiveness of human service agencies.

OBM is not a cure-all or a quick fix for the many challenges and difficulties facing human services. It cannot fundamentally alter society's priorities or create resources where none exist. However, it is a tool that can improve the effectiveness of human service personnel. It is a systematic and well documented approach that can reduce cost, improve productivity, and help organizations achieve

Portions of this paper were presented in a symposium entitled "Organizational Behavior Management: Application to the Human Services," Jon P. Ziarnik, Chairman, Association for Behavior Analysis, Milwaukee, May, 1982.

desired goals. It is a well documented, effective approach, but it is not a magic cure. Implementing effective change is challenging. OBM will not make it easy, but does make it possible.

The purpose of this article, then, is threefold. First, we will discuss the nature of human service agencies with emphasis on those characteristics that create special challenges to the improvement of staff effectiveness. Next we will review the nature of OBM. What is it? What are its major contributions, the basis of its effectiveness? Finally, we will outline the future for applying OBM in human service settings. How should the tasks be approached? What are the most significant opportunities and challenges?

THE NATURE OF HUMAN SERVICES

Human service institutions are in a critical phase of their development. While the nation remains committed to the values of the system, there is a growing consensus that the conservative and efficient use of resources is imperative. The expectation is that the system should be administered in an accountable, business-like fashion. Yet several characteristics of human service organizations make this expectation far from simple.

The Bottom Line Problem

The costs associated with human service delivery are very tangible. We can quite easily specify the amount of money that goes into providing particular services. By contrast, assessing the value of what comes out of a human service organization is quite difficult. Most commercial organizations value their product on the basis of demand: What will the market pay for a particular output? Human service organizations, however, often operate somewhat apart from the free market system (Welch & Hammaker, 1983). Services are often reimbursed indirectly through government expenditures, or third party payment or are provided within regulated systems. Put another way, the direct beneficiary of the service is typically not purchasing it in the same way one purchases a hamburger or a pair of shoes. This precludes direct valuation of the services provided.

In the absence of such a direct measure we often face the prospect of indirectly valuing outcome. What is the value of rehabilitating a felon? What is the value of reducing loneliness? Or, at the extreme, what is the value of a human life? While these outcomes can be quantified, they are subject to a great deal of debate, debate based on individual values and personal relevance. (That is, are we discussing the value of life in general or your life in particular?) Because of these problems, the value of human services is not typically measured in monetary terms. The possibility certainly exists that some system of valuation could be developed; however, this is an exceedingly complex and long term project (Warner, 1979).

The Input/Output Problem

Another fundamental problem facing human services is that there is often an unknown relationship between the inputs made by staff (such as the number and type of therapy sessions delivered, the number of interactions by a case worker, the duration of interventions, etc.), and the output (that is, desired client outcomes). This uncertainty arises on two levels. On one level, many of the interventions have an unknown effect. In many areas of human services we cannot say that a given staff behavior will have a given impact on a client. On a second level, the outputs themselves are varied and diverse. Outcomes are sometimes good in some respects and poor in others. They often do not vary on a single, easily quantified dimension. Further, it is not clear that everyone agrees on what the specific outcomes ought to be (Hansenfeld & English, 1978).

Further complicating the problem of relating organizational inputs to outputs is the difficulty of an extensive time scale. In many human service settings, the desired outcome is the prevention of some unwanted consequence (e.g., a crime, early death, disability, mental illness, etc.). Determining the effectiveness of prevention efforts poses several problems. Proving the success of prevention efforts requires either a crystal ball, or alternatively, long range, well controlled studies. By definition, these studies require a long time scale. The effectiveness of human service providers cannot really be judged until sometime in the future.

The Organizational Purpose Problem

One of the most challenging problems facing human service organizations is the problem of contradictory goals. Almost all human service organizations have avowed, publicly stated goals. Often, these are global, nonspecific, and positive. For example, phrases such as "restoring an individual to the level of highest independent functioning" or "helping clients achieve their maximum potential" are widely used in official publications and formal presentations. Appropriately, these goals are typically consistent with the values held by individual staff members and administrators. Such goals have been referred to as the manifest functions of human service organizations (Kaswan, 1982).

However, human service organizations also fulfill many unacknowledged, yet socially mandated functions. Examples of such functions include social control and socialization, removal of undesirable individuals from the public view, keeping certain individuals out of the labor force, and so on. These goals have been referred to as the latent functions of human service organizations (Kaswan, 1982).

The problem arises that manifest and latent goals are often diametrically opposed. For example, a particular mental health institution might have a manifest goal of getting patients discharged and living at least semi-independently in the community. In opposition to this goal is the goal of the many citizens in the community who prefer to have these individuals in the institution where they will not encounter them on a day to day basis. As the institution becomes more effective at achieving its manifest goal, it comes into increasing conflict with society's desire for it to fulfill its latent goals. As courts increasingly demand the mode of least restrictive care, citizens of communities rebel at having the mentally ill live with them in the community. This problem, although seldom discussed, is very real. It has, for example, been identified in the health, human service, educational and penal systems (Kaswan, 1982; Szasz, 1970; Winett & Winkler, 1972; Schur, 1973).

The Idealistic Staff Problem

Many individuals entering the human service field do so to serve humanity. On many levels it is indeed a plus to have dedicated and caring staff. Yet such a staff does present some problems. When such staff encounter the realities of low funding levels, demanding and unappreciative clients, the elusive nature of their goals, and other harsh day to day realities, they become prime candidates for burn out, absenteeism, turn-over and other forms of organizational withdrawal (e.g., Tuttle, 1983; Patrick, 1982; Cherniss, 1983).

Idealism can more easily be replaced with pessimism than with a realistic view of the role that staff play in the human service endeavor. Such a tendency to develop pessimism limits the ultimate development of effective, realistic approaches for meeting important human service needs.

The Numbers Problem

This problem arises as a result of some of the other problems mentioned above. While human service agencies typically do not have specific measurable outcomes that can be effectively tracked, there still needs to be some system for reimbursement. This has historically led to a default solution, that of payment based on the amount of service delivered rather than on the effectiveness of that service. Specifically, agencies are reimbursed for the number of client visits, the staff hours involved in the service, or the specific procedures used. In short, they are reimbursed based on delivering service rather than on having an impact.

The inevitable consequence of this default solution is that agencies and organizations tend to pursue those things for which they receive reimbursement (cf. Harshbarger & Maley, 1974). The quantity or duration of service often looms larger than the quality or effectiveness. Activity is often pursued at the expense of outcome. While many in the system defend this approach, it only makes matters worse. It results in a pseudo bottom line that obscures possible input/output relationships, diminishes staff morale, and glosses over conflicting organizational purposes.

THE NATURE OF ORGANIZATIONAL BEHAVIOR MANAGEMENT

What is OBM? And how can it make an important contribution to the management of staff behavior in human service settings? This section will answer these questions. One formal definition of OBM is offered by Frederiksen and Lovett (1980):

> OBM is the application of the principles of behavioral psychology and the methodologies of behavior modification/applied behavior analysis to the study and control of individual or group behavior within organization settings. (p. 196)

From this definition several things are immediately apparent. First, OBM shares the common purpose and general subject matter of most other approaches to behavior in organizations. That is, it is concerned with both the understanding and management of behavior in organizations; it has both a theoretical and a practical mission. In addition, the subject matter is the behavior of individuals and groups in organizational settings. These characteristics are shared with a host of related areas such as industrial psychology, organizational development, and management theory.

However, the definition also highlights two important respects in which OBM differs from other approaches. First, it is primarily based on a behavioral or operant psychology framework. This can be contrasted to other approaches which are based on cognitive theories, personality theories, expectancy theory, or the like. The most widely acknowledged theoretician contributing to this position is B. F. Skinner. His work has set the stage for behavior analysis from which OBM has developed. While it is safe to say that the theoretical base of OBM has broadened substantially from a strict operant or behavioral approach, it is also important to acknowledge its roots.

A second divergence of OBM from other approaches is the use of the methodology of behavior modification/applied behavior analysis. As we shall discuss below, this methodology differs in several fundamental respects from the approaches traditionally used to evaluate behavior in organizations. These differences have important implications for both theoretical understanding and practical day-to-day management of organizational staff.

Major Contributions

There are four major contributions of organizational behavior management (see Frederiksen & Johnson, 1981, and Frederiksen, 1982 for more detailed discussion). These contributions form the basis for using OBM to improve staff effectiveness in human service settings.

The first of these contributions is the *theoretical perspective*. As introduced above, OBM is based primarily on behavioral or operant psychology. As the field has evolved over recent years, it has broadened somewhat to include the influences of social learning theory, (e.g., Davis & Luthans, 1980) as well as behavioral systems analysis (Krapfl & Gasparotto, 1982; Morasky, 1982). The adoption of these related theoretical perspectives has been important for two important reasons.

First, adopting a behavioral perspective allowed access to a large body of already available research. The data from operant or social learning psychology allow one to make predictions and understand relationships that might otherwise go unnoticed. For example, saying that a leader's behavior serves as a discriminative stimulus allows one to make predictions about how to establish "leadership," how one might become a leader, etc., (Davis & Luthans, 1979; Scott & Podsakoff 1982). While subsequent research may ultimately show that these theoretical predictions are inaccurate, having access to these perspectives gives one a solid place to start. A second and somewhat related benefit of this theoretical perspective is that it tells one what to focus on in the organizational setting. Organizations are complex places. Those who wish to make changes in an organization must begin by focusing their attention on some aspect of this complexity. Is one to look first at the personalities of the organizational members? Their cognitive style? Expectancies? The theoretical perspective associated with OBM tells us that we must first look at the employees' behavior. What is it that they are actually doing? This is not a focus on what they think about what they are doing as much as it is a focus on what their actual behavior *is*. We must also focus on the context in which that behavior occurs. What events or situations immediately precede the behavior and what consequences follow it? Here again the emphasis is on the immediately preceding and following events, not the historical context or long term consequences of a behavior. This elegantly simple tool provided by the behavioral perspective has proven to be immensely practical in simplifying inherently complex situations. In other words, it tells observers where to focus their attention within that complexity we call an organization.

The second important contribution is the *methodology* of applied behavior analysis. In many ways this may be the single most important contribution that OBM has to offer. Applied behavior analysis methodology is unique in several respects (Baer, Wolf, & Risley, 1968; Hersen & Barlow, 1976; Luthans & Davis, 1982). First is its insistence on ongoing measures of actual behavior rather than on single assessments of how people respond to a test. OBM insists that the actual behavior of importance be assessed in the natural environment as it actually occurs rather than in an artificial testing situation. Further, OBM requires that these measures be taken continuously rather than at one or two points. The importance of this requirement is hard to overestimate. It forces us to look at what is actually happening, on an ongoing basis, in the situation of relevance. Inferences relating our measurements to the actual behavior are thus eliminated. Further, any trends in performance are immediately obvious, as are delayed effects of our interventions.

A related methodological requirement is the use of single-case rather than between group research methodology. Several excellent discussions of single-case methodology are available elsewhere and will not be duplicated here (Hersen & Barlow, 1976; Komaki, 1982). However, the important point that single-case methodology relies on a demonstration of functional control over behavior rather than statistical control should be emphasized. In other words, researchers must demonstrate that the intervention they are evaluating has a practical impact on behavior, rather than simply demonstrating statistical significance. Further, this methodology eliminates a need for control groups, a feature that is immensely practical in actual organizational settings.

A third major contribution of OBM is a *body of hard data*. A number of extensive literature reviews (Andrasik, 1979; Babb & Kopp, 1978; Frederiksen & Johnson 1981) have shown that OBM has accumulated a relatively large volume of well-controlled experimental studies. These studies are almost exclusively conducted in organizational settings, using employees as subjects. They are generally well controlled and have demonstrated positive outcomes. Importantly for our current topic, about half of these studies have been conducted in human service settings. Thus OBM has already accumulated an important data base that can be drawn upon for managing human service settings. Individuals wishing to improve staff effectiveness in human service settings do not have to start from scratch. A number of approaches have already been well documented in the literature and give one a head start.

A fourth and final major contribution of OBM is *techniques for behavior change*. The field has developed, tested, and documented the effectiveness of several techniques that have consistently been shown to change important staff behavior in organizational settings. The importance of this is that OBM not only helps us understand behavior, it also gives us effective tools for managing it. Many of these techniques are illustrated in the current volume. However, some of the key ones include the use of goal setting and performance feedback, positive reinforcement, behavior based training strategies, and the important, emerging area of self-management.

It should be noted that these techniques share names that may be familiar to many readers. For example, it is not uncommon for people to say "we already use feedback." However, the similarity in terminology should not be confused with the actual techniques. In many organizations the term feedback means a meeting with the supervisor, on a quarterly or semiannual basis, in which the individual's performance is critiqued based on supervisor's impressions, survey results, or average performance. In contrast, OBM based feedback techniques are quite different. Feedback occurs on a daily or weekly basis rather than quarterly. In addition it is based on people's actual performance rather than on supervisor's impressions or survey results. Finally, it specifically addresses a single targeted behavior rather than a global evaluation that includes a wide variety of behaviors. In other words, it pinpoints the specifics of what is being done well and what improvements remain to be made, rather than providing a generalized impression. A similar set of distinctions holds when we talk about positive reinforcement. Reinforcement in an OBM intervention is often of a small magnitude, keyed to specific performance, and is contingent. Thus, like behavioral feedback, it tends to be given frequently and immediately. The presentation of the reinforcement depends on the behavior of the individual. This is in contrast to the reward systems in most organizations, which are dispensed more on the basis of people simply showing up for work rather than their performance when they are there.

Here again the significance of this contribution is that these are techniques that have demonstrable effectiveness in changing specific staff behaviors. In other words they work. The key, of course, is selecting the appropriate behavior for change.

APPLYING OBM TO HUMAN SERVICE ORGANIZATIONS

OBM offers one overriding promise to human service organizations. That is, an effective and reliable approach to changing specific staff behaviors. A variety of OBM techniques, including goal setting and feedback, contingent reinforcement, training, and self-management have been shown to effect improvement in important staff behaviors (Frederiksen & Johnson, 1981). These have been replicated across a wide variety of settings by a wide variety of settings by a large number of investigators. However, there is an important key to unlocking staff effectiveness: the key is to target the appropriate behavior for change.

In some circumstances it may be relatively easy to determine the best target. There are some staff behaviors that are extremely critical to given organizations. The situation described by Robins and Lloyd (1984) provides an example. In this particular instance staff attendance at work was clearly a pivotal behavior for the overall functioning of the organization. Likewise, other organizations may have other key staff behaviors that *must* occur if the organization is to be successful. Yet it is far too easy to assume that we know what the key behaviors are rather than to determine them on empirical basis.

The study by Johnson and Frederiksen (1984) makes the point. Even though the administration of the particular human service organization in question had long assumed that the delivery of a particular type of therapy would improve outcome, this was demonstrated not to be the case. The administration had not made an unreasonable assumption because this type of therapy had been shown to be "effective" by other investigators. Yet the demonstration of effectiveness in one setting does not necessarily translate to the fact of effectiveness in another. Put another way, the effectiveness of staff behavior must be assessed and not assumed.

The usefulness of OBM in changing specific staff behaviors forces human service organizations to fact an important challenge. This challenge is clearly specifying what goals will be pursued. As we discussed in the first section, human service organizations face the dilemma of pursuing both manifest and latent goals, goals that can be at odds with one another. Unfortunately neither the manifest nor the latent goals are typically operationalized with enough precision to permit careful tracking. If it is to be maximumly effective, OBM puts a special requirement on organizations. That requirement is that they must come to grips with what primary and secondary goals will actually be pursued. This is often a difficult task for human service organizations to face. It requires that they come to grips with not only their manifest goals, but also with their often unacknowledged latent goals. Further, these goals must be stated with enough specificity so they can be clearly operationalized and reliably measured. The difficulties and potential rewards of such specification is demonstrated in the study by Elder, Sundstrom, Brezinski, Waldeck, Calpin, & Boggs (1984). Community mental health centers have been directed to reduce unnecessary client dependence on the human service system, a laudable, but vague goal. By operationalizing one aspect of this goal as medication dependence, the authors were able to target staff behaviors relevant to achieving the goal.

By itself, OBM does not give human service organizations any guidance as to what the content of the goals should be. That guidance must come from the staff, administration, governing bodies, the community, and society at large. All OBM does is force the issue. However, the careful specification of goals allows a second key element of an OBM approach to come into play.

That second element is the continuous tracking of outcomes. The actual data on how well the organization is attaining all of its goals (even though they may be conflicting or diametrically opposed) must be gathered in a continuous manner. It is not sufficient to look at outcome once or twice a year. Rather, there should be some accumulation and updating of data on a month by month or even week by week basis. Of course, it is not possible or practical to do this for every specific organizational goal. However, it is important to monitor a large number of key goals. The reason for an insistence on ongoing data collection is that it allows the management to determine the extent to which key goals are being met day in and day out. It gives the organization a bottom line against which to measure the effectiveness of new programs, innovations, and staff performance. While the case for tracking relevant outcomes has been well argued in other places (e.g., Gilbert, 1978), there are several specific advantages that need comment.

By virtue of giving human service organizations an ongoing bottom line continuous tracking of outcomes also sets the stage for establishing clearer input/output relationships. Programs that alter staff behavior can be evaluated with respect to their effect on significant organizational outcomes. Clearly, increasing staff activity is not at all synonymous with improving organizational outcome. A footracer running in the wrong direction is worse off than one who is at the starting line. By the same token a program designed to increase a staff activity that has little impact on significant organizational outcomes is probably worse than no program at all. Such a program drains precious resources that could be applied for other purposes.

Here again the methodology available in OBM has an important role to play. By virtue of single-case experimental methodology and small scale evaluation designs it is possible to pilot test programs before they are put into full scale operation. This piloting permits a determination of possible impact on important organizational outcomes (assuming that those outcomes have been operationalized and are also being tracked on an ongoing basis).

Finally, management faces the challenge of making human service organizations effective in turbulent, rapidly changing times. While there seems to be ample justification for optimism regarding the ability of OBM to improve staff effectiveness, the reality of a turbulent environment confronts many human service organizations. Even the best thought-out OBM program can be rendered useless should a major change occur in the human service organization's external environment. The challenge, then, is to create approaches that are not only effective, as OBM clearly is, but are also extremely adaptable. For example, there may be a need to concentrate more on self-management programs for institutional staff than on administration centered programs. In any event, programs must be developed with regard for their flexibility and adaptability over time and changing circumstances. While this additional demand may be unfortunate, it is all too characteristic of the environment that human service organizations must operate in.

CONCLUSION

In this paper we have argued that OBM has much to offer human service organizations. It is an approach to managing staff behavior that works. If implemented appropriately it can have an important impact on staff effectiveness.

However, this implementation is not a simple task. Human service organizations face a variety of challenging problems. They do not have a commonly agreed upon bottom line, often operate without clear relationships between staff inputs and organizational outcomes, run a high risk of staff burnout, and are often faced with socially imposed, incompatible goals. These and other problems have all too often resulted in human service organizations playing the numbers game. That numbers game often takes the form of such inquiries as "How much did we do?" "How many people were seen?" or "How much service was delivered?" rather than "What was the impact that was made?"

Even in view of these problems, OBM has some important contributions to make. It can help force the issue of establishing measurable organizational goals and tracking them on a continuous basis. If this is done, it will allow a human service organization to establish a relevant bottom line that can be monitored for many important purposes. Such continued monitoring will allow OBM to be used to improve staff effectiveness and produce desired outcomes rather than simply increase well intentioned but ineffective activity. The OBM literature in general and this volume in particular present some clear examples of how this impact might work.

Yet OBM clearly does not provide all the answers. While it can help get the most out of available resources it cannot, in and of itself, generate new resources. Likewise, we have much to learn with regard to the side effects of interventions, the acceptance and maintenance of programs, and management in a turbulent environment.

We recognize these as prospects and opportunities for OBM rather than barriers. We also recognize that the human service system is undergoing a fundamental transition. To continue its contribution to the nation's well being, foresighted, systematic and effective management will be necessary. OBM stands ready to accept the challenge.

REFERENCES

Andrasik, F. (1979). Organizational Behavior Modification in business settings: A methodological and content review. *Journal of Organizational Behavior Management*, *2*, 85-102.

Baer, D.M., Wolf, M.M. & Risley, T.R. (1968). Some current dimensions of Applied Behavior Analysis. *Journal of Applied Behavior Analysis*, *1*, 91-97.

Babb, H.W., & Kopp, D.G. (1978). Application of behavior modification in organizations: A review and critique. *Academy of Management Review*, *3*, 281-292.

Christian, W.P. (1984). A case study in the programming and maintenance of institutional change. *Journal of Organizational Behavior Management*, *5*, 99-152.

Cherniss, C. (1983). *Staff burnout job stress in the human services*. Beverly Hills: Sage publications.

Davis, T.R.V., & Luthans, F. (1979). Leadership reexamined: A behavioral approach. *Academy of Management Review*, *4*, 237-248.

Davis, T.R.V., & Luthans, F. (1980). A social learning approach to organizational behavior. *Academy of Management Review*, *5*, 281-290.

Elder, J., Sundstrom, P., Brezinski, W., Waldeck, J.P., Calpin, J.P., & Boggs, S.R. (1984). An organizational-behavioral approach to quality assurance in a community mental health center. *Journal of Organizational Behavior Management*, *5*, 17-35.

Frederiksen, L.W., & Johnson, R.P. (1981). Organizational Behavior Management. In M. Hersen, R.M. Eisler & P.M. Miller (Eds.), *Progress in behavior modification*. New York: Academic Press.

Frederiksen, L.W. (1982). OBM: An overview. In L.W. Frederiksen (Ed.), *Handbook of organizational behavior management*. New York: Wiley.

Frederiksen, L.W., & Lovett, S.B. (1980). Inside Organizational Behavior Management: Perspectives on an emerging field. *Journal of Organizational Behavior Management*, *2*, 193-204.

Gilbert, T.F. (1978). *Human competence: Engineering worthy performance.* New York: McGraw-Hill.

Harshbarger, D.D., & Maley, R.F. (1974). *Behavior analysis and systems analysis: An integrative approach to mental health programs.* Kalamazoo: Behaviordelia.

Hasenfeld, Y., & English, R.A. (1978). *Human service organizations.* Ann Arbor: University of Michigan Press. 1-25.

Hersen, M., & Barlow, D.H. (1976). *Single case experimental designs: Strategies for studying behavior change.* New York: Pergamon.

Jensen, C.C., Morgan, P., Orduno, R., Self, M.A., Zarate, R.G., Meunch, G., Peck, D., Reguera, R.A., & Shanley, B. (1984). Changing patterns of residential care: A case study of administrative and program changes. *Journal of Organizational Behavior Management, 5,* 153-172.

Johnson, R.J., & Frederiksen, L.W. (1984). Process vs. outcome feedback and goal setting in a human service organization. *Journal of Organizational Behavior Management, 5,* 37-56.

Kaswan, J. (1982). Manifest and latent functions of psychological services. *American Psychologist, 36,* 290-299.

Komaki, J. (1982). The case for the single case: Making judicious decisions about alternatives. In L.W. Frederiksen (Ed.) *Handbook of organizational behavior management.* New York: Wiley.

Krapfl, J.E., & Gasparotto, G. (1982). Behavioral systems analysis. In L.W. Frederiksen (Ed.), *Handbook of organizational behavior management.* New York: Wiley.

Luthans, F., & Davis, T.R.V. (1982). An idiographic approach to organizational behavior research: The use of single experimental designs and direct measures. *Academy of Management Review, 1,* 380-391.

Maher, C.A. (1984). Description and evaluation of an approach to implementing programs in organizational settings. *Journal of Organizational Behavior Management 5,* 69-98.

Morasky, R.L. (1982). *Behavioral systems.* New York: Praeger.

Patrick, P.K.S. (1982). *Health care worker burnout. What it is, what to do about it.* Chicago: Inquiry.

Robins, J., & Lloyd, M. (1984). A case study examining the effectiveness and cost of incentive programs to reduce staff absenteeism in a pre-school. *Journal of Organizational Behavior Management, 5,* 173-187.

Schur, E.M. (1973). *Radical non-intervention.* Englewood Cliffs, N.J.: Prentice Hall.

Scott, W.E. Jr., & Podsakoff, P.M. 1982. Leadership, supervision and behavioral control: Perspectives from an experimental analysis. In L. W. Frederiksen (Ed.), *Handbook of organizational behavior management.* New York: Wiley.

Szasz, T.S. (1970). *The manufacture of madness: A comparative study of the inquisition and the mental health movement.* New York: Harper and Row.

Tuttle, T.C. (1983). Organizational productivity: A challenge for psychologists. *American Psychologist, 38,* 479-488.

Warner, K.E. (1979). The economic implications of preventive health care. *Social Sciences and Medicine, 13C,* 227-237.

Welch, J.D., & Hammaker, M.K. (1983, April). *Increasing competition to reduce health care costs: An old antitrust concept.* Virginia Bar News.

Winett, R.A., & Winkler, R.L. (1972). Current behavior modification in the classroom: Be still, be quiet, be docile. *Journal of Applied Behavior Analysis, 5,* 499-504.

Section II:

DEVELOPING APPROACHES TO EFFECTIVENESS

An Organizational Behavior Management Approach to Quality Assurance in a Community Mental Health Center

John P. Elder
Philip Sundstrom
William Brezinski
John P. Waldeck
James P. Calpin
Stephen R. Boggs

ABSTRACT. Current mental health service delivery models emphasize minimizing the dependence of clients on mental health systems as a part of assuring service quality. The present study focused on one step along the independence-dependence dimension; that of deciding whether to treat anxious or depressed clients with out-patient counseling alone or outpatient counseling plus psychotropic medication. Alterations in referral procedures were used to reduce staff's inappropriate referrals to psychiatrists for purposes of medication. While 60% of all newly admitted anxious or depressed clients were medicated during baseline, only 18% of the new clients presenting these symptoms were medicated during intervention. Results are discussed in terms of the need to develop clear guidelines for quality assurance in mental health services, and the practical and ethical implications of implementing such programs.

Within a health care context, Quality Assurance (QA) may be defined as administrative interventions designed to remediate deficien-

The authors would especially like to thank Tom Parker, Dwight Harshbarger, Lynn Artz, Lee Frederiksen and David Abrams for their invaluable assistance in the conceptualization of research design and analysis; Perry Bosmajian and Steve Lovett for helping with the data collection, and Mary Marcos for manuscript preparation.

Data from this study were presented at the World Congress on Behavior Therapy, Washington, 1983.

For reprints contact John P. Elder, Pawtucket Heart Health Program, The Memorial Hospital, Pawtucket, RI 02860.

19

cies in health service provision. Steps involved in QA programs include the identification of potential problem areas, the selection of a data source and specification of variables, the collection of baseline data, interventions to correct deficiencies, and reassessment (Palmer & Nesson, 1982). QA programs have recently been or soon will be mandated for evaluations of the structure, process and/or outcome of all publicly supported health and mental health services (e.g., Farrington, Felch, & Hare, 1980; Palmer & Nesson, 1982).

Medical models of mental health service delivery are characterized by passive "patients" and authoritarian professionals, a late treatment focus, and subsequent dependence of patients on the mental health system (Jason & Glenwick, 1980, p. 8). During the late 1960s and 1970s, a variety of writings decrying the dependence of clients on the mental health system appeared. Concurrently, financial resources for mental health services diminished (e.g., Albee, 1969; Anthony & Hall, 1972; Szasz, 1970; Polack & Kirby, 1976; Pasamanic, Scarpitti, & Dinetz, 1967). This combination of factors resulted in a redefinition of quality of care and the development of alternative mental health service delivery models such as the Balanced Service System.

The Balanced Service System (BSS) incorporates tenets of behavioral and community psychology in providing a conceptual framework for the delivery of mental health services (Melville, Kibler, & Haddle, 1977). Through the machinery of the Joint Commission on the Accreditation of Hospitals (JCAH, 1976) the Balanced Service System prescribes procedural and clinical guidelines for community mental health operations and the assurance of their quality.

The principles of the BSS focus on the efficiency and quality of service delivery. Efficiency issues include whether the clients have been referred to an appropriate service, how quickly such a referral is acted upon, how punctually and completely requisite paper work is finished, and how expensive services are. Quality variables, according to BSS proponents, involve measures of clinical rather than administrative efficiency with an emphasis on clients' independence from the mental health system.

Unfortunately very few practical suggestions for obtaining this goal of systems independence are suggested by the Balanced Service System's authors. Neither JCAH nor the BSS literature provides clear operational definitions of systems dependence or specific guidelines for reducing systems cost. Nor do they set forth support techniques for changing staff behavior to comply with new or existing guidelines. Organizational behavioral procedures, such as the systematic applications of instructions, incentives, modeling, feedback and other consequation of staff behavior may be required to successfully move an organization toward its goal (e.g., Andrasik, 1979; Frederiksen & Johnson, 1981).

In community mental health centers, any organizational or procedural alterations including QA programs must carefully consider "political" strategies for dealing with firmly entrenched practices standing in contradiction to CMH goals. The current lack of clarity in BSS and similar guidelines obligates state-level or community mental health staff to operationalize BSS principles for their own local service delivery systems and QA programs.

The present study was conducted in a mental health center where no clear expectancies of clinicians' behavior had been established. Neither systematic staff supervision nor in-service training was integrated within the center's typical operation. Although lip service to general BSS principles was paid by the center's Administration, no commitment to the redirection of resources or functions was evident. While all staff demonstrated general concern for client "outcome," we lacked a framework for agreeing on what constituted appropriate process, let alone positive outcome. This lack of quantifiable, consensus-based goals, limited our ability to respond to changing external regulations which in turn were too vague to elicit an appropriate, timely response.

The present study's authors employed BSS guidelines in developing a QA program for a four-county community mental health center. The three general phases in the development of this quality assurance program included: (a) operationalization of the dimensions of minimum-maximum systems dependency; (b) determination of where on this dimension to intervene; and (c) development of organizational-behavioral procedures such as staff training and systematic contingencies to reduce the client's dependency on the mental health system.

This present study targeted one aspect of the quality dimension of Quality Assurance. The issue of efficiency was not addressed in this intervention. Specifically, this study is an evaluation of an attempt to change staff referral behavior. Corresponding client outcome measures were collected to assess the impact of this change on system dependency.

METHOD

Setting and Subjects

The present study was conducted in a rural four-county mental health center in Central Appalachia, an area relatively isolated from major urban and academic centers. The Center's catchment area included a population of approximately 140,000. Individuals referred to the Center for mental health treatment came from nearly all economic and educational levels, although the majority of the clients fell within the lower socio-economic stratum. Client problems ranged from maladjustment reactions to behavioral disturbances requiring institutionalization.

In each of three county offices involved in the present study, the staff was divided into multidisciplinary treatment teams. Treatment team leaders were three Master's degree-level psychologists, one social worker and one pre-Master's degree counselor who were responsible for supervising three to seven treatment team members each. Team members included registered nurses, bachelor and master level psychology specialists, counselors, and various paraprofessional staff. Two county offices (counties "A" and "B") had two treatment teams each while the third county (County "C") had one.

The 21 subjects of the present study were all staff with full or partial outpatient responsibilities. This included the two treatment team leaders plus five staff in County A, the two team leaders plus nine staff in County B, and the team leader and two staff in County C. Nurses and after care workers who provided services to post-institutionalization clients were excluded.

Psychiatric services were provided by one full-time and three consulting psychiatrists. Psychiatrists had extremely large case loads and saw clients very briefly (for as little as 4 minutes), primarily for purposes of medication prescriptions, reviews and evaluations. Seemingly insurmountable problems in recruiting a complete contingent of full-time psychiatrists was a constant factor in the administration of the Center.

In spite of the psychiatrists' large caseloads and traditional medical orientations, outpatient staff had long been accustomed to routinely referring nearly all clients for psychiatric consultations, which normally resulted in medication prescriptions. Drugs prescribed to "neurotic" clients included flurazepam, clorazepam, meprobamate, cloriazepoxide, oxazepam, diazepam, and hydroxine for "anxiety"; amitriptyline, desipramine, nortriptyline, doxepin, imipramine, and protaiptyline for "depression"; and various manufacturer combinations of the above for "agitated depression."

Procedure Operationalization

In response to state directives to implement a Balanced Service System model for accreditation, the supervisory staff of the mental health center proceeded to review all existing Balanced Service System and Joint Commission literature in order to determine the critical accreditation steps. While JCAH guidelines are relatively clear on how to set up record keeping and other administrative procedures, considerable ambiguity was encountered in determining how to increase clients' "independence," reduce "systems penetration," and otherwise enhance clinical quality. Therefore, the treatment team leaders and their supervisors developed objective definitions of the critical concepts of the Balanced Service System, especially that of "systems dependence."

The first step in developing these operational definitions was to determine where the bulk of present and former clients fell on various points of the systems dependence dimension. All existing agency programs were also ranked on these dimensions. "Maximum dependence" programs were defined as those that involved higher levels of cost to the agency and required minimal independent behavior of the client. Programs classified as requiring minimum dependence were those which relied heavily on the clients' personal resources as well as those of alternative community agencies, and were of relatively low cost to the agency. The Center's programs for both severely impaired and general outpatient clients were then ranked on this dimension. The ensuing "systems dependence" model is depicted in Figure 1.

Intervention Decision

The bulk of the systems dependence elements depicted in Figure 1 were either already being addressed or were beyond the scope of the Center's administrative control (e.g., the decision of whether to institutionalize following brief unsuccessful hospitalization). Moreover, although the reasons for referral to psychiatrists were for "medication screening" rather than medication per se, over 60% of

FIGURE 1. Community Mental Health Services ranging from Minimum to Maximum Systems Dependence.

anxious and depressed clients referred for screening were given anti-anxiety or anti-depression prescriptions. Given these factors a decision was made to attempt a reduction in the number of outpatients referred for psychotropic medication. The staff believed that the rate of referrals for medication evaluation could be reduced, especially for clients diagnosed "neurotic-anxious" or "neurotic-depressed." In light of the evidence that such problems may stem more from specific skill deficits than from biogenic disorders and the success of non-pharmacological (Bassuk, Schoonover, & Gelenberg, 1983) and specifically behavior therapy procedures for dealing with anxiety (e.g., Wolpe, 1958; Bernstein & Borkevec, 1973; Suinn & Richardson, 1971) and depression (e.g., Rehm, 1977; Zeiss, Lewinsohn, & Munoz, 1979; Beck, Rush, Shaw, & Emery, 1980), the administrative staff deemed the then current incidence of medication prescriptions too costly, intrusive and inclined to create dependency.

That minor tranquilizers commonly used for the treatment of anxiety can create "dependency" is fairly widely documented. The use of minor tranquilizers may produce physical and psychological tolerance, and has the potential for toxic side effects (Julien, 1975, pp. 42-65; Bassuk et al., pp. 184-185). While anti-depressant medications have not been shown to produce physical tolerance, their use must still be closely monitored by highly trained medical professionals (Julien, 1975, pp. 268-271), especially given their potential toxicity (Bassuk et al., 1983, pp. 39-50). This requirement in turn promotes the dependence of the client on the mental health system.

Implementation

Techniques for reducing the medication rate included a two-phase process. First, the five treatment team leaders and sixteen staff were given intensive training and decision algorithm guidelines for treating anxiety and depression without medication. Staff were trained to assess biophysical problems and thought disturbances and were instructed to continue to refer clients with these problems to the psychiatrists. For clients with depressive symptoms, staff were given detailed instructions on assessing suicidal potential and biogenic disorders. Again, the routine of referring clients in these categories was retained. Detailed written guidelines for both the behavioral assessment and treatment of anxiety and depression were provided.

In the second phase, the treatment team leaders reviewed the above information with their staff at weekly individual and group supervision meetings. Supervisors modeled appropriate behavior by staffing their own cases at meetings and demonstrating how such techniques could apply.

A second element of this phase further prompted changes in the behavior of the therapists. Any therapist wishing to refer to a psychiatrist had to present their prospective client's case to fellow staff both before and after they implemented at least four sessions of a behavioral self-control treatment regimen (i.e., relaxation/stress management anxiety reduction techniques modeled after Bernstein and Borovec (1974) and others; self-control and social skills training procedures taken from Rehn (1977) and others for reducing depression). If at the end of this four-week period they felt their client still could benefit from psychotropic medication, they were required to present the case again in the weekly group supervision meeting as though it were a new case. If no referral was desired, brief, occasional updates were all that were required for ongoing reporting.

Design

The study employed a "multiple baseline across settings" design (Hersen & Barlow, 1976) using percent of admissions with medication as the dependent variable. Settings were three of the four county offices of the community mental health center. (Due to the small size of the fourth office's operation [2 staff] and distance from the main center, it was not included in the intervention study.) The entire time frame of the study was twenty-four weeks, with the County A intervention beginning after eight weeks of baseline, County B after 10 weeks, and County C after 12 weeks.

Given the amount of detail to be imparted during the first phase of the intervention, staff training in behavioral assessment and therapy for anxiety and depression was begun at a time corresponding to the beginning of baseline. Weekly training sessions in these and related topics were conducted in each county office for 1-1/2 to 2 hours. Written summaries of each training session's content were left with staff. Two short answer examinations were also administered, with corrective feedback provided by the Service Director. A general expectancy that we eventually wanted to prioritize behavioral over medical treatments was established.

One-week to ten days before the beginning of the intervention, the referral decision algorithms were shared with and the procedural changes announced to the staff, with the specific dates they were to begin. Staffing changes and team leader modeling began the first week of the intervention. No new training material was provided to Counties B and C after the County A intervention had begun. Training continued in all counties throughout the intervention period, with the emphasis shifting to skill refinement through case presentations by all staff.

Measures

Data collection. A determination of diagnosis was made using the Diagnostic and Statistical Manual of the American Psychiatric Association (DSM-II) guidelines for assessing neurotic anxiety and depression. Intake summaries and progress notes served as source material for these determinations. As no systematic method for recording such information had yet been implemented, each clinician had a somewhat unique charting approach. Raters, therefore, had to be thoroughly familiar with the use of the DSM-II.

Medication. Medication decisions were monitored through checks of the medications page of the chart. This source was deemed optimally reliable in that its use was legally required for administering medications.

Client outcome. To determine whether the administrative changes actually had an effect on systems dependence and other indices of client outcome, several additional variables were assessed. Specifically, the *number of therapy sessions* held, *client change* as measured by the Global Assessment Scale, and the *disposition* of the client were assessed upon the conclusion of the study.

Sessions and disposition were obtained directly from the client's chart. Of particular interest were clients who had been in the system for a considerable period of time, indicating a dependence on the services provided. Twenty sessions was selected as the cutoff point between excessive and non-excessive utilization of services. (This figure was selected as it was the midpoint of a large separation of these data.)

Client change was assessed via the Global Assessment Scale (GAS; Spitzer, Gibbon, & Endicott, 1973). The GAS combines ordinal and ratio scales to form a 100 point rating of current functioning. The rater was instructed to rate the client's entry functioning level after reading the intake interview, and then to read all progress notes and discharge summary and provide a rating of functioning upon termination.

The disposition of the client upon termination was recorded directly from the chart's termination sheet. Dispositions were categorized as "terminated because of illness, death or move"; "refused further service"; "did not notify center of reason of termination" or "no further service needed."

RESULTS

Reliability

Admissions data were collected by the first author who reviewed all charts for new referrals during the baseline and intervention periods. All new referrals were classified into one of the five categories i.e., "neurotic-anxiety" and "neurotic-depression" with or without medication, and diagnoses other than anxiety or depression. The first author made these categorizations after the intervention and without knowledge of whether the clients entered treatment during baseline or intervention phases. Reliability was checked by a pre-doctoral psychology graduate student unconnected with the present study. The reliability for the categorizations was *Kappa* = 0.78. GAS ratings were made by a psychology graduate student without knowledge of the treatment phase. GAS reliability was checked by an ABD staff psychologist on 50% of County A's cases. Reliability for the GAS ratings was *Kappa* = 0.89. Reliability was also computed between these two raters on number of sessions and disposition. Agreement was perfect on these variables.

Medication Rates

The major results of the study are displayed in Figure 2. The percent of admissions with medications for anxiety and depression and the number of new admissions are graphed for each of the three county offices. In County A, ten of the eleven clients (91%) admitted for anxiety or depression during baseline were medicated. During intervention only 5 of 32 (16%) were medicated for these same presenting problems. In County B, eleven of 21 clients (55%) received medication for anxiety or depression during the baseline phase. This was reduced to only 7 of 28 (27%) during intervention. Finally in County C, 8 of 16 (50%) clients received medication upon being admitted for anxiety or depression during baseline while none of the 7 admitted during intervention received such medication. (Much of County C's lower baseline medication rate can be attributed to the fact that their psychiatrist was on vacation during the seventh two-week period, leaving them without routine psychiatric coverage for that period of time.) The overall reduction in medication was from 60% in baseline to 18% during intervention.

The medication reduction reflects a change in staff's referral rates rather than in psychiatrists' prescriptions. Of the anxious or depressed clients who were referred to psychiatrists during intervention, three-fourths received medication. This figure corresponds closely to baseline rates.

Six month follow-up data taken during a six week period were available for Counties B and C. During this period ten of 26 clients

Percent of admissions with medication

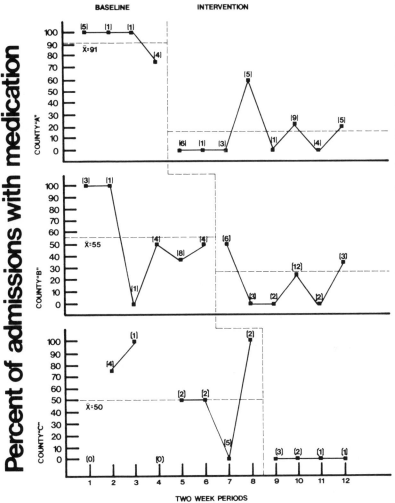

FIGURE 2. Percent Admissions with Medication per two week periods. (Ns are in parentheses.)

in County B (38%) were medicated upon admission. Of the two anxious/depressed clients admitted in County C during this period, neither were medicated. The intervention's effects, therefore, seemed to be maintained over time.

Client Outcome

The interpretation of client outcome data is greatly limited by three factors: (1) data are incomplete; (2) data are primarily derived from reviews of clients' charts rather than directly obtained; and (3) data are indirectly rather than causally related to the study's independent variable. Of the 143 clients monitored during the study, only 109 of their charts were accessible for extracting outcome data. The unavailability of older, primarily "baseline" charts, due to record keeping problems unconnected with the present study *per se*, especially contributed to this shortfall. For example, in County A, none of the 11 baseline charts were available for review. The 70% of the charts which were reviewed represent a large but certainly non-scientific sample.

The fact that change scores were extracted from therapists' written, subjective accounts of client behavior also limits their interpretability. Although extracted ratings did prove to be reliable, their validity is of course questionable, only in part assured by the therapists being unaware that changes would eventually be reviewed.

Twenty percent and 35% of the medicated clients during baseline and intervention phases, respectively, (27.5% of all medicated clients) were seen for more than twenty sessions. In contrast, only 7% (baseline) and 11% (intervention), or 10% of all non-medicated clients, were seen in excess of 20 sessions.

Early discharge (dropout) data however, favored the medicated clients. Only 59% (baseline) and 10% (intervention), or 7.5% of the medicated clients failed to return after three or fewer therapy sessions. In contrast, 35% (baseline) and 53% (intervention), or 51% of all non-medicated clients did not return after three or fewer sessions. When all early discharge clients are eliminated from analyses, however, medicated clients still received excessive amounts of service in nearly twice as many cases as non-medicated clients.

Treatment efficiency may be conceptually defined as the effectiveness per resources expended to achieve the effect. In the present case, this would involve dividing Global Assessment Scale change by the number of treatment sessions. Interestingly, non-medicated baseline clients demonstrated the most change in the fewest number of treatment sessions. Both intervention groups required more effort for a modest change, with the efforts involving medicated clients in this phase being by far the least efficient. All non-medicated clients averaged 6.9 units of change or 0.78 units per session, while medicated clients averaged total changes of 7.0 or only 0.6 units per session.

The most common disposition involved termination after no notification from the client of any reason for not returning. However, both the medicated and non-medicated intervention groups included more clients who were discharged after further care was not indicated (i.e., an apparent treatment success) than did their baseline counterparts. No notable differences between the combined medicated groups and the non-medicated groups was forthcoming.

No objective measure of staff satisfaction with the procedural changes was available. It was interesting to note, however, that only one of the 25 staff affected complained that the procedures were unnecessarily "anti-medical" and possibly even harmful. All other staff appeared (in many cases enthusiastically) receptive to the changes.

DISCUSSION

The present study demonstrated the efficacy of a Quality Assurance procedure for reducing "systems" (and medication) dependence in a community mental health center. The procedure involved three general stages: an operationalization of the concept of "systems dependence," a determination of where along the continuum of systems dependence this particular community mental health center's programs most needed attention, and development of procedures for altering the clinical behavior of the center's outpatient staff (i.e., staff training, modeling, and consequation of compliance/non-compliance with the program).

Although the study's Quality Assurance program emphasized service process over structure or outcome (cf. Palmer & Nesson, 1982), outcome data were collected to determine whether post-treatment indicators of systems dependence and related variables were associated with the study's manipulation. The interpretation of outcome date was seriously limited by reliance on charts, incompleteness, and indirect association with the independent variable. However, our conclusion that the reduction in medication rates was tantamount to decreasing systems dependence was at least corroborated by the fact that fewer non-medicated than medicated clients received "excessive" amounts of treatment. This assertion, however, is attenuated by the higher early dropout rate of the clients who did not receive medication following the onset of the intervention and the conflicting picture presented by Global Assessment Scale changes and client dispositions.

In general, the treatment outcome picture indicates that the manipulation may have produced a positive although certainly more varied result than the prior clinical approach. With the exception of the resulting higher dropout rates, the intervention was at least not contraindicated. The enhancement of counselors' clinical skills may have also benefited those who received medication.

Two general reasons may be postulated for the success of the medication intervention. First, the administrative manipulation employed may have been sufficiently powerful itself to impact the staff's referral patterns. Such uses of rather straightforward antecedent (i.e., staff training) and negative consequence manipulations of staff behavior have been proven effective elsewhere in the mental health literature (e.g., Kreitner, Reif, & Morris, 1977; Epstein & Wolff, 1978; Lovett, Bosmajian, Frederiksen, & Elder, 1983). However, such attempts have largely focused on administrative procedures (e.g., record keeping) which may seem relatively unimportant to the clinical staff involved.

While training provided by supervisors may be necessary to effect initial staff behavior change, they may not be sufficient to maintain it. In the present study's baseline phase, attempts to modify attitudes and knowledge through orientation to the Balanced Service System and general staff training in behavior therapy techniques were ineffective in reducing referrals for psychotropic medication. However, subsequent procedural reviews, prompting and modeling by treatment team leaders, continued staff training emphasizing non-drug therapeutic trials for certain diagnoses, and implementation of a consequation procedure both elicited and maintained the desired change. As the staff tried the new approaches and apparently discovered their utility with clients who stayed in treatment, very little subsequent prompting was required. Supervisors were approached more frequently for information on other behavior therapy techiques than for permission to refer clients to staff psychiatrists, potentiating a generalization of therapeutic skills to areas other than those targeted within the present study. Future studies in this area should include and even focus on measures of staff abilities as well as typical indices of client outcome.

The present study looked at only one aspect of modifying systems dependence, that involving the decision whether to medicate outpatient clients presenting with anxiety or depression. Similar procedures should be tested at other points in the dependence continuum for both outpatient and chronically impaired clients (e.g., by intensifying efforts in day programming and partial hospitalization to reduce inpatient use). It appears that such efforts should focus on enhancing the competence of staff actually operating the program. Other studies may want to include specific, behavioral measures of client outcome (e.g., securing/retaining employment, freedom from legal involvement) which could be causally linked to clinical or CMH procedures. Procuring such data will eventually be necessary to justify major procedural alternatives, especially potentially controversial ones.

The "baseline" of the present study was contaminated in that staff began training during this eight to twelve week period. The assumption was made that staff training alone would be insufficient to alter referral behavior, an assumption largely borne out by the baseline data. Other researchers, however, may be interested in evaluating a "true" baseline wherein absolutely no intervention was carried out, or in comparing different combinations of training, supervision, modeling, and consequation. Logistical and institutional constraints, however, will generally limit research efforts in this area.

As a result of our experiences, we would also like to offer suggestions to those who develop guidelines for designing and/or evaluating mental health services. Such guidelines, although admirable in their exhortations for client advocacy, minimizing dependence and reducing costs, currently provide little in the way of practical, uniform procedures for achieving these goals. By developing objective decision steps along the systems dependence dimension we were able to create clear guidelines. It is of course conceivable that others may disagree without operationalization. However, the bulk of the outcome data appear to support our attempt to create a treatment environment that relied more on the skills and orientation of the primary therapists and less on medication.

Effective guidelines for assuring clinical quality must be far more specific regarding relevant process and outcome variables. They must also take into account the unique problems of mental health systems in implementing such guidelines. Without better specification, future accreditation processes may continue to focus on relatively trivial structural variables, administrative rather than staff behavior, and to create confusion for those attempting to improve clinical services. Entrenched, maladaptive practices will survive such "quality assurance."

REFERENCES

Albee, G. (1969). Emerging concepts of mental illness and models of treatment: The psychological point of view. *American Journal of Psychiatry*, (7) *125*, 870-876.

Andrasik, F. (1979). Organizational behavior modification in business settings: A methodological and content review. *Journal of Organizational Behavior Management*, *2*, 85-102.

Anthony, W., & Hall, M. (1976). The efficacy of psychiatric rehabilitation. *Psychological Bulletin*, *78*, 447-456.

Bandura. A. (1977). *Social learning theory*. Englewood Cliffs, New Jersey: Prentice-Hall.

Bassuk, E., Schoonover, S., & Gelenberg, A. (1983). *The practitioner's guide to psychoactive drugs*. 2nd Ed. New York: Plenum Press.

Beck, A. T., Rush, J. A., Shaw, B. F., & Emery, G. (1979). *Cognitive therapy of depression*. New York: The Guilford Press.

Bernstein, P., & Borkovec, T. (1974). *Progressive relaxation training: A manual for the helping profession*. Chicago, Illinois: Research Press.

Epstein, L., & Wolff, E. (1978). A multiple baseline analysis of implementing components of the problem-oriented medical record. *Behavior Therapy*, *9*, 83-88.

Farrington, J., Felch, W. J., & Hare, R. (1980). Quality assessment and quality assurance: The performance review alternative. *New England Journal of Medicine*, *303*, 154.

Frederiksen, L., & Johnson, R. (1981). Organizational behavior management. M. Hersen, R. Eisler, & P. Miller (Eds.), In *Progress in behavior modification*. New York: Academic Press.

Hersen, M., & Barlow, D. H. (1976). *Single case experimental designs: Strategies for studying behavior change*. New York: Pergamon.

Jason, L., & Glenwick, R. (1980). *Behavioral community psychology: Progress and prospects*. Glenwick and Jason (eds.). New York: Praeger Press.

Joint Commission on Accreditation of Hospitals. (1976). *Principles for Accreditation of Community Mental Health Service Programs*. (Suppl) Chicago, J.C.A.H.

Julien, R. (1975). *A primer of drug action*. San Francisco: Freeman and Co.

Kreitner, R., Reif, W. E., and Morris, M. (1977). Measuring the impact of feedback in the performance of mental health technicians. *Journal of Organizational Behavior Management*, *1*, 105-109.

Lovett, S., Bosmajian, P., Frederiksen, L., & Elder, J. P. (1983). Procedural alterations and performance feedback in enhancing treatment quality of outpatient mental health services. *Behavior Therapy*, *14*, 170-177.

Melville, C., Kibler, K., & Haddle, H. (1977). *The balanced service system*. Atlanta, Georgia: Georgia Mental Health Institute.

Palmer, R., & Nesson, H. (1982). A review of methods for ambulatory medical care evaluations. *Medical Care*, *20*, 758-781.

Pasamanic, B., Scarpitti, F., & Dinetz, S. (1967). *Schizophrenics in the community: An experimental study of the prevention of hospitalization.* New York: Appleton Century, Crofts.

Polak, P., & Kirby, M. (1976). A model to replace psychiatric hospitals. *Journal of Nervous and Mental Disease, 162*, 13-22.

Rehm, L. P. (1977). A self-control model of depression. *Behavior Therapy, 8*, 787-804.

Spitzer, R., Gibbon, & Endicott, J. (1973). *The global assessment scale.* Unpublished.

Suinn, R., and Richardson, F. (1971). Anxiety management training. A nonspecific behavior therapy program for anxiety control. *Behavior Therapy, 2*, 498-510.

Szasz, T. S. (1970). *The myth of mental illness.* New York: Harper & Row, 1970.

Wolpe, J. (1958). *Psychotherapy by reciprocal inhibition.* Stanford, California: Stanford University Press.

Zeiss, A., Lewinsohn, P., & Munoz, R. (1979). Nonspecific improvements effects in depression using interpersonal skills training, pleasant activity schedules, or cognitive training. *Journal of Consulting and Clinical Psychology, 47*, 427-439.

Process vs Outcome Feedback and Goal Setting in a Human Service Organization

Richard P. Johnson
Lee W. Frederiksen

ABSTRACT. This study examined the effects of process behavior feedback and goal setting for staff of a human service organization on those process behaviors and intended outcomes. The effects of outcome feedback and goal setting on outcomes intended and specific process behaviors were also studied. Process feedback was found to markedly increase the rate of process behavior but had no effect on intended outcomes. Outcome feedback had no effect on either intended outcomes or the related process behaviors. The implications of these results for the selection of appropriate targets for organizational interventions are discussed.

The effects of performance feedback and goal setting on organizational behavior has been demonstrated in a variety of human service settings, across a broad spectrum of behaviors, and with subjects differing on a number of important dimensions (Frederiksen & Johnson, 1981). The focus of research in this area has typically been concerned with increasing the frequency of staff process behaviors such as conducting therapeutic sessions intended to generate a specific outcome such as client improvement. For example, Pommer and Streedback (1974) provided feedback and rewards for staff completion of posted duties in a residential center for emotionally disturbed children. They found the combination of public posting of

This research served as partial fulfillment for the first author's Doctor of Philosophy degree from Virginia Polytechnic Institute and State University. The authors wish to thank Dr. R. Michael Marsh, Superintendent of Catawba Hospital and the staff for their support, ideas, and encouragement in the completion of this project. Correspondence should be directed to the first author, Northeast Community Center for MH/MR, Roosevelt Blvd. and Adams Ave., Philadelphia, PA 19124.

37

duties and feedback/incentives to be superior to public posting or feedback and incentives alone. Similarly, Maher (1981) evaluated a feedback and goal setting intervention designed to increase the number of teacher consultations and behavioral programs implemented by two school psychologists. A dramatic increase in both of these targeted behaviors was noted upon introduction of the feedback and goal setting package. However, in both of these studies there was no documented impact on client outcome.

A few studies have demonstrated the effectiveness of feedback and goal setting for increasing the rate of attaining valued organizational outcomes. Such a study was reported by Pomerleau, Bobrove, and Smith (1973). Monetary rewards were provided to staff of a psychiatric institution whose assigned patients improved the most as measured by a behavioral checklist. This was compared to a condition where similar rewards were provided to staff voted by their peers as most cooperative. Patient improvement as measured by the behavioral checklist was great under the condition which provided incentives for staff with the patient making the greatest gains, but no patient progress resulted from the condition where incentives were available for staff voted most cooperative. No data was reported for the specific staff process behaviors required to generate such improvement in patient behavior however.

A few studies have evaluated the effects of feedback and goal setting interventions on both staff process behaviors and outcomes intended, but the target of the intervention has generally been limited to the process behavior. Illustrative of this approach was an investigation reported by Ivancic, Reid, Iwata, Faw, and Page (1981). The focus of the intervention was language training for profoundly retarded institutionalized children. During and following language training sessions, staff were provided with feedback by their supervisors for the rate of appropriate staff antecedent vocalizations, descriptive praise and sound imitations and prompts. Feedback related to patient vocalizations was also provided. The intervention package resulted in increases in both appropriate staff behavior and patient vocalizations.

The results of these and other studies seem to make it clear that feedback and goal setting interventions can result in increases in desired process behaviors and organizationally relevant outcomes. However, no study has yet clearly evaluated the effect of process feedback on those process behaviors *and* intended outcomes and, conversely, the effect of outcome feedback on organizationally relevant outcomes *and* related process behaviors.

The purpose of the present research was to examine the effects of providing feedback and goal setting for process behavior on those process behaviors and related outcomes in a human service organization. Feedback and goal setting for outcomes and the subsequent effects on those outcomes and related staff process behaviors were also examined.

METHOD

Setting and Subjects

This study was conducted at a state mental health institution which serves geriatric patients aged 60 years or older. As an organization, it had a capacity of 250 patient beds. There were approximately 270 staff members with about 40% (110) of those employees being involved in direct nursing care. Patients were most frequently admitted as transfers from other state psychiatric institutions and tended to be chronically mentally ill. Many of the patients, presumably due to their age, had associated with their diagnoses some form of organic brain disorder.

There were a total of five treatment units with approximately fifty patients on each unit. Administrative supervision was provided by the superintendent of the hospital. Other primary administrative personnel included the director of nursing care, a medical director, and a coordinator of mental health services. A staff of psychologists, social workers, and adjunctive therapists provided treatment support services in conjunction with five medical doctors. Approximately 20-25 direct nursing care staff were assigned to each of the patient treatment units.

The subjects for this study were the direct care nursing staff of each of the five patient units. Individual nursing personnel of the day shift and the evening shift were involved in the research study. These were the shifts during which patients were expected to be active and awake. The direct care nursing staff of the institution consisted of four types including psychiatric aides, licensed practical nurses, registered nurses, and head nurses.

Intervention Targets

The primary program emphasis at this hospital was the Reality Orientation (RO) of the patients. Specific program protocols, had been designed for use with the patients. The titles of these RO programs included Newscheck Program, Newspaper Program, Group Conversation, Morning Meeting and Evening Meeting, and a more basic Reality Orientation Program. All of these programs shared the goal of orienting patients to reality. More specifically, RO has been defined as "a structured communication device designed to assist disoriented persons recover their feelings and perceptions about person, place and time" (Folsom, 1978). Detailed and specific instructions on the conduct of these programs had been published and were available on each treatment unit in the form of a program manual (Grant, 1977). The RO group sessions were conducted by direct care nursing staff throughout the day.

The group sessions themselves were highly verbal in that discussions about specific topic areas were led by the assigned nursing staff member(s). The nursing staff would elicit comments from and attempt to facilitate conversation among the patients present at the group sessions. The information presented during these RO groups by the nursing staff would be repeated several times during each group. The common elements stressed in all RO group sessions was threefold: (1) orientation of patients to who they and others were; (2) orientation to where the patients had been, currently were and would be in the future; and (3) orientation to recent, remote, and future events.

The process behaviors required to produce improved RO among the patients in this institution primarily involved nursing staff exposing patients to the content of the RO programs described above. Patients were encouraged, but not required, to attend RO group programs. Direct care nursing staff were expected to conduct RO group sessions but no specific number of groups or number of patients involved in those was required.

The outcome intended as a function of these process behaviors was the improved RO of the patients. This increase in orientation to person, place and time was important to the stated mission of the hospital in rehabilitating patients for placement in settings less restrictive than a state hospital.

Dependent Measures

Process behaviors. Process behaviors were defined for the purposes of this study as the daily total number of nursing staff contacts with patients in RO group sessions. This figure was determined by adding the number of patients present in each RO group conducted for that day. Patients included in more than one daily RO group were counted each time they were included in another RO session. Staff contacts with patients in RO groups could vary as a function of the number of RO groups conducted or the number of patients in each RO group. It was required that a group session be conducted for ten or more minutes to be counted as an RO group session. Staff were required to follow the general protocol for that particular type of RO group.

A form was employed to determine the number of patient contacts with staff in all groups for each treatment unit. Staff were instructed to complete these forms for each group, regardless of the content of the group session, at the time the group was completed. The completion of this form was identified as a requirement by the superintendent of the hospital, and included information such as number of patients and staff present, type of group and time and place. The director of nursing was required to implement its use. No distinction was made between types of groups to be recorded and no effort was made to identify RO groups as the measure of concern.

Data sheets for patient group sessions were collected by the nurse in charge of each shift for each patient unit and taken to the director of nursing. The completed forms were then given to one of the authors for compilation each day. No other personnel were allowed access to this data after the forms had been collected.

The reliability of data collected concerning patient RO group sessions was determined by having two staff psychologists directly observe RO groups and note the same information as nursing unit staff were required to provide. This information was independently recorded and no comparison between nursing staff and staff psychologist was permitted.

Reliability data was collected for 3.93% or 169 of the total 4313 RO groups conducted during the 98 days of data collection. Additionally, 144 reliability observations of non-group occurrences were made. The lowest percent of agreement for group occurrence observed was 92.11 with an overall average reliability of 95.8%. Observations of group nonoccurrences were in agreement an average of 91.6% of the time.

Agreement for the number of patients reported to be in each group was also determined. All but one patient unit (i.e., PFU-1) over-reported the number of patients per group. However, this over-reporting of the number of patients in a group was evenly distributed across conditions. That is, over-reporting did not increase as a function of implementing treatment conditions. Although the patient count for staff and reliability observers exactly agreed 27.16% of the time, the rate of agreement plus or minus one patient was substantially higher at 48.15%.

Data collection—Process behaviors. A form was employed to determine the number of patient contacts with staff in all groups for each treatment patients in RO groups could vary as a funciton of the number of RO groups conducted or the number of patients in each RO group. It was required that a group session be conducted for ten or more minutes to be counted as an RO group session. Staff were required to follow the general protocol for that particular type of RO group.

Outcomes Intended

The outcomes were measured as the number of correct, or oriented patient responses to questions posed by staff members. These questions were designed to assess orientation to person, place, time, and past and recent events. Correct responses to these questions were considered to be indicative of patient orientation whereas incorrect responses were reflective of disorientation. Four questions were presented to ten patients selected from each of the five treatment units daily, Monday through Friday. The questions were randomly selected from two lists of eight questions each, with two questions coming from each list. List One consisted of questions designed to assess orientation to self and immediate surroundings such as "How old are you?" and "What is today's date?" List Two questions were considered more difficult and related to remote events and awareness of distant surroundings such as "Who is President of the United States?" These questions were selected because they were typical of those used in psychiatric institutions to assess mental status and orientation to reality. Since ten patients from each of the five treatment units were asked four questions daily, 40 was the maximum daily RO score that could be obtained for any given treatment unit.

Adjunctive Therapy (AT) staff members presented the questions to patients to determine daily RO. These AT staff members were responsible to the coordinator of mental health services (the first author) and were not aware of the purpose of the study. The questions to be used for each day were prepared in advance by a secretary and were distributed to AT staff each morning. Patients to be questioned were randomly selected by the same secretary from a prepared list of current residents such that each patient was queried at least once each week.

The reliability of data collected from the daily patient question responses was determined by having a second staff member simultaneously record the responses from the same patients. Patient responses were independently recorded and observer agreement was later calculated. No attempt was made to resolve discrepancies at the time of the data collection.

Reliability data for patient RO was collected for an average of 19.76% of the 5390 patient interviews or an average of 34.69% of the 108 patient RO observation days. The rate of agreement was determined by dividing the total number of observation agreements by the total number of reliability observations made. The lowest rate of agreement was 93.7% and the overall average was 95.8%.

Procedure

Baseline. Data sheets for patient group sessions (Process) were simply collected and tabulated for this phase of the study. No information concerning the number of patient contacts in group sessions with staff members was provided to any hospital staff member at this time and no goals were established. Responses to questions concerned with the group session data sheets indicated that the completion of these data sheets was required by the superintendent of the hospital.

Adjunctive Therapy staff submitted their reality orientation data collection sheets daily to one of the authors. No information was provided to any hospital staff members concerning the accumulated data and Nursing Department personnel were not made aware of any connection between the collection of the patient orientation data and RO group session information. Questions concerning the daily patient RO questions were answered by indicating that patients' levels of functioning were being assessed.

Treatment Procedures—Process Feedback

Nursing staff of two patient units, Process Feedback Unit 1 (PFU-1) and Process Feedback Unit 2 (PFU-2), were introduced to the feedback intervention with the following explanation presented by the coordinator of mental health services:

Reality Orientation and news awareness are important independent living skills that will aid functioning in the community. We all know that the RO programs are effective ways of teaching these skills for the elderly group with whom we work. These graphs will help you to know the number of patient contacts in daily RO instructional sessions for at least ten minutes each. Already displayed on this graph is the information for patients engaged in such sessions over the past few days. Do you have any questions?

Also displayed on this two by three feet graph was a one-quarter inch wide horizontal red line indicating a goal for the number of patient group contacts to which the staff of that unit should aspire. The goal established for each unit was fifteen percent above the baseline levels of daily patient RO contacts in group sessions.

The only questions which were asked concerned the meaning of the data to be posted on the graphs and the consequences of not reaching the established goals. Explanations of the data were provided and staff were assured that not attaining the goals would result in no adverse consequences.

A general discussion also followed concerning ways of increasing the number of patient contacts in RO group session. The Head Nurse for each PFU was present when the instructions were presented.

Data concerning the number of patient contacts with staff in RO groups were provided daily for each unit by posting on the graphs which were displayed prominently in the center nursing station of each patient unit. Baseline data were included on the graphs for three weeks prior to the implementation of the treatment.

Treatment Procedures—Outcome Feedback

Two other patient units, Outcome Feedback Unit 1 (OFU-1) and Outcome Feedback Unit 2 (OFU-2) received instructions concerning outcome feedback as follows:

One of the most important goals of patient rehabilitation is to teach Reality Orientation and attention to recent news events. However, there are many ways this can be done. Often, it is helpful to know how many patients are actually oriented to reality or aware of recent news events. These graphs will show you the number of oriented responses for patients received from questions posed to them each day, out of a maximum of 40 possible such responses. The information for the past few days is already posted on these graphs for your information. Do you have any questions?

As for the previous groups, a detailed explanation of the graphs and the meaning of the data followed the presentation of these instructions. Staff then discussed ways they might increase patient RO. Some of these staff initiated suggestions included providing incentives for patients with increased RO, working more frequently with patients individually or in groups, and encouraging more patient interaction. The Head Nurse was present during these discussions.

These graphs were also displayed in the center nursing office. Data were posted on the graph for patient orientation daily. Three weeks of baseline data for patient orientation was displayed on the graphs.

The graphs for the OFU nursing units also had a one-quarter inch wide horizontal red line drawn to indicate a goal to be attained for patient orientation. This line was drawn at a point twelve and one-half percent above the mean percent of the oriented responses obtained during baseline. Goals were chosen because they were thought to be challenging, but not impossible.

Comparison group. One patient unit served as a Comparison Unit (CU) for the purposes of this study. Data concerning patient orientation and patient contacts in RO group sessions was collected throughout the study but no feedback was presented to staff for either measure. No graphs were present on the unit and no presentation was made to this unit regarding the study.

Research Design

A multiple baseline design across patient treatment units (Hersen & Barlow, 1976) with a comparison unit was employed to evaluate the effects of the interventions. This design was used in preference to a treatment withdrawal design for two reasons. First, if desirable treatment effects were obtained as a result of the intervention, the hospital administration would not be likely to approve withholding of the intervention for research purposes. Second, it was not clear that the treatment intervention could be fully withdrawn once implemented. That is, feedback, goal setting, and the instructions provided may have continued to influence performance even after being withdrawn. Therefore, a multiple baseline design across treatment units was selected. Figure 1 shows the research design employed for this study.

RESULTS

Process Feedback Effects on Process Behavior

The results for the two program units that received feedback concerning patient RO group contacts (i.e., PFU-1 and PFU-2) along with patient RO group contact data from the CU are presented in Figure 2. This figure also presents the 95% confidence intervals for each weekly mean. These figures were calculated to determine changes in the overall mean. The range of this confidence interval means that about 95% of the time, a mean score would fall in this range due to random variation (i.e., chance) alone. Therefore, if these intervals overlap extensively from baseline to treatment, then the treatment cannot be considered to have produced an effect on the dependent measure. Although there are no clear criteria for estab-

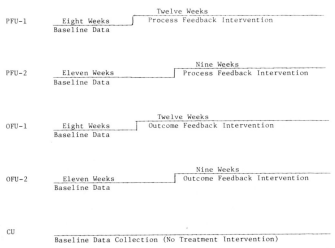

FIGURE 1. Experimental Design (PFU-Process Feedback Unit; OFU-Outcome Feedback Unit; CU-Comparison Unit).

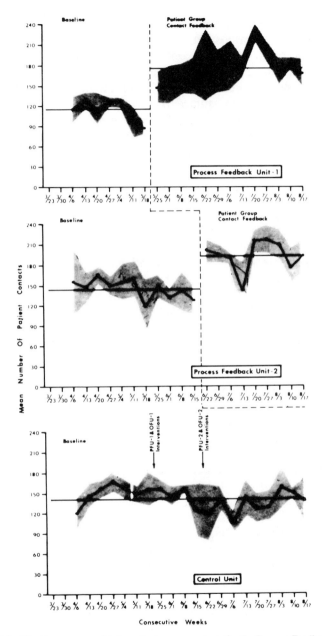

FIGURE 2. Weekly averages of daily patient group contacts for the Process Feedback Units and the Comparison Unit. Note: Shaded areas indicate 95% confidence intervals.

lishing the degree of minimum overlap required to determine an effect, the fewer overlaps between baseline and treatment mean confidence intervals, the more confident one can be that the treatment did produce an effect on that variable.

The baseline or treatment average of patient RO group contacts for each unit was determined by dividing the number of patient group contacts by the number of observation days in the baseline or treatment condition. PFU-1 averaged 116.59 contacts during baseline compared to 174.30 contacts during the process feedback condition. Similarly, the baseline mean for PFU-2 patient group contacts was 146.72 compared to a treatment mean of 199.64. By way of comparison, no increases in patient RO group contacts were noted in the data of the CU. A relatively stable rate of patient RO group contacts ($\bar{X} = 142.37$) was obtained throughout the 20 weeks of the data collection.

Two possible strategies were available to staff to increase the number of patient contacts in RO groups. First, the number of actual groups conducted could be increased. Second, the number of patients included in each group could be increased. Marked increases in the number of RO groups conducted occurred with the introduction of process feedback for both PFUs while no change occurred within the CU. PFU-1 and PFU-2 averaged 10.78 and 9.07 groups per day, respectively, during baseline. This mean figure increased to 14.42 for PFU-1 and to 12.36 for PFU-2 during the process feedback intervention. A comparatively stable rate of daily RO groups conducted was obtained for the CU which had a weekly average of 7.40 RO groups per day.

By way of contrast, no noticeable changes were observed in the daily number of patients per group for PFU-1, PFU-2 and the CU. A slight increase over the baseline mean of 11.14 to 12.32 patients per group was noted for PFU-1. However, PFU-2 actually registered a slight decrease from 16.19 patients per group during baseline to 15.88 during the process feedback intervention. The weekly number of patients per group for the CU was 19.31 with no noticeable variations from one time period to another.

To summarize, substantial increases in the rate of staff process behavior (i.e., patient RO group contacts) were observed upon the introduction of process feedback for both PFU-1 and PFU-2. No such increase was observed for the CU which received no feedback. Both PFUs increased the average daily number of RO groups conducted while the CU maintained a stable rate of daily RO groups.

No unit registered noticeable changes in the average number of patients included in each RO group.

Outcome Feedback Effects on Intended Outcomes

Figure 3 shows patient orientation for OFU-1, OFU-2, and the CU. It should be noted that the OFU-1 was effectively disbanded the week of July 13 to allow for renovation of the living quarters. Consequently, only half of the original number of patients remained intact. Average weekly patient orientation for OFU-1 during the nine weeks of baseline ($\bar{X} = 28.49$) did not noticeably differ from patient orientation during the weeks this program unit remained intact and experienced the outcome feedback intervention ($\bar{X} = 29.42$). Similarly, OFU-2 received an average daily patient orientation score of 15.40 during baseline compared to 16.13 during the outcome feedback treatment conditions. The CU patient orientation scores remained stable and averaged 23.12 for the 22 weeks of data collection.

While slight increases in patient orientation scores were obtained for both OFUs, the confidence intervals overlapped consistently. Thus, the variation obtained in daily patient RO scores was so great as to suggest that these slight increases were random variations not attributable to the intervention.

In summary, outcome feedback was not associated with change in RO among patients of OFU-1 or OFU-2. Patient RO scores from the CU did not noticeably change throughout the course of this study.

Process and Outcome Effects on the Targeted Variable

Two additional questions posed concerned the effects of outcome feedback and goal setting on process behavior and, conversely, the effects of process feedback and goal setting on outcomes intended. With respect to the first of these questions, Figure 4 presents the number of patient RO group contacts for OFU-1 and OFU-2, neither of which received process feedback. Up to the week of July 13, patient RO group contacts actually declined slightly on OFU-1. An overall mean of 138.14 daily patient RO group contacts was obtained during the time period OFU-1 was intact. A stable pattern on results was obtained for OFU-2 where the mean number of daily pa-

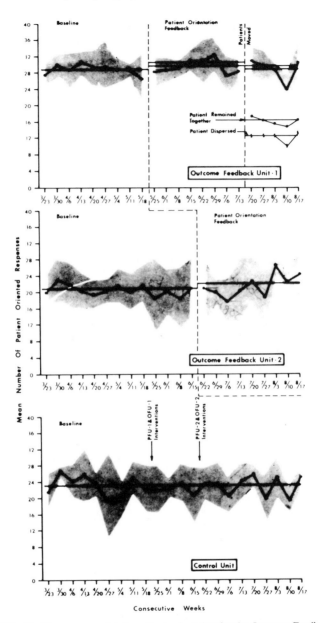

FIGURE 3. Weekly averages of daily patient orientation for the Outcome Feedback Units and the Comparison Unit. Note: Shaded areas indicate 95% confidence intervals.

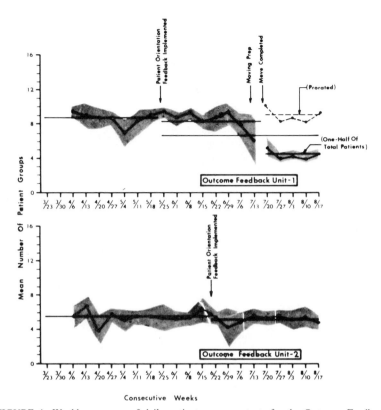

FIGURE 4. Weekly averages of daily patient group contacts for the Outcome Feedback Units. Note: Shaded areas indicate 95% confidence intervals.

tient RO group contacts was 85.79. No consistent increase or decrease in the rate of group contacts was apparent.

The RO scores obtained for PFU-1 and PFU-2 patients are presented in Figure 5. No noticeable changes occurred in those patient RO scores over time. Patients of PFU-1 obtained a mean RO score of 14.64 while those from PFU-2 had a daily average RO tally of 26.52. The confidence intervals for both of these units overlapped markedly throughout all 22 weekly data points.

To summarize, outcome feedback did not appear to effect process behavior for either of the OFUs. Likewise, process feedback produced no gains in the outcomes intended for the process feedback units.

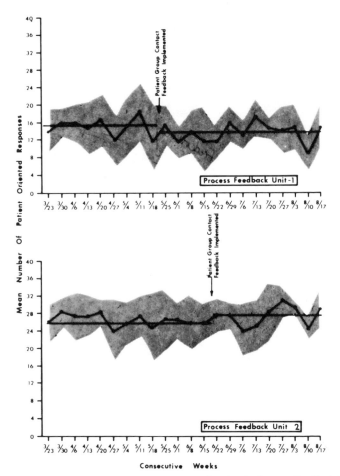

FIGURE 5: Weekly averages of daily patient orientation for the Process Feedback Units.
Note: Shaded areas indicate 95% confidence intervals.

DISCUSSION

The most definitive conclusion that can be drawn from the results of this study is this: feedback and goal setting for staff process behaviors, defined as patient RO group contacts, produced increases in the occurrence of those behaviors. No such increases in staff process behavior were observed for either the CU, or OFU-1 and OFU-2 which received only outcome feedback.

The results of the outcome feedback and goal setting intervention were not impressive. Only slight increases in patient RO were observed for OFU-2 after implementation of orientation feedback, and essentially no change was found in RO for OFU-1. No change was found in RO during identical time periods for the CU. Reality orientation for PFU-1 declined somewhat while the patients of PFU-2 were only slightly more oriented, even though no RO feedback was presented.

The effects of process feedback and goal setting on outcomes intended and, conversely, of outcome feedback and goal setting on process behavior were nil. Thus, within the context of this study, one type of feedback (e.g., process) produced no predictable change in the other measure (e.g., outcomes intended).

The fact that predicted changes in process behavior occurred as a function of process feedback and goal setting, but that no changes in intended outcomes were observed as a result of outcome feedback and goal setting, could have been due to a number of factors. Some of these include staff variables or variables related to the feedback system.

With respect to the staff variables, a lack of training, motivation or perception of control over patient orientation could account for the results. However, required readings and in-service training seminars insured proper training. Motivation to improve patient RO was evident in the verbal responses of staff to patient RO improvements and openly expressed disappointment in response to patient RO decline. But studies from human service settings which have demonstrated the effects of outcome feedback and goal setting on organizational outcomes also usually provided concrete rewards as incentives for staff for outcome improvements (e.g., Hollander, Plutchik, & Horner, 1973; Iwata, Bailey, Brown, Foshee, & Alpern, 1976; Pomerleau et al., 1973). Since no praise or tangible reward component was included in this intervention, it is possible that the combined goal setting and feedback did not provide sufficient motivation for change in the outcomes intended.

A perceived lack of control of patient RO is a more plausible explanation since there was no individual staff assignment system for each patient's RO. However, staff on all of the patient units were assigned daily to conduct RO groups. This created an individualized system of accountability for conducting RO groups while only a group responsibility system existed for patient RO. Support for this possibility comes from Emmert (1978) who demonstrated that both types of feedback (i.e., group and individual) were effective in increasing desired outcomes, but individual outcome feedback was superior to group outcome feedback.

An important feedback system variable that may have influenced the obtained results is the relationship of the process variable to the intended outcome. Published studies have demonstrated the effectiveness of RO in producing changes in patient orientation (e.g., Barnes, 1974; Harris & Ivory, 1976). However, while the staff and administration of the institution believed that RO groups, conducted according to the prescribed protocols would produce desired changes in patient RO, this belief was not empirically verified by the results of this study.

The unfounded belief in program effectiveness in this situation is not unlike that found in many human service agencies. For example, the professional staff of mental health clinics are usually expected to engage in a variety of process behaviors, such as group and individual therapy, intended to produce the outcome of client improvement. However, outcomes produced as a result of these staff process behaviors are rarely evaluated (Harshbarger, 1979). Perhaps more importantly, outcomes resulting from specific processes are even less frequently evaluated within the context of a given agency. While feedback provided to staff concerning process behaviors resulted in the increased performance of those process behaviors, the outcomes which should have resulted may not have occurred due to the lack of a relationship between the two (c.f. Frederiksen, 1982).

There are many limitations to the interpretation of the results of this study. First, interpretations must be limited to the population of nursing staff which served as subjects for the study. Second, the leadership of the patient units was vested in five head nurses. It is reasonable to expect that they differ on a number of leadership style dimensions. Third, the type of patient residing in this setting is also a moderating factor in the interpretation of these results. All were geriatric patients, and most were chronically mentally ill. Finally, this study was implemented and evaluated within only one organizational setting. Different organizations using the identical methodology might find results very different from those obtained in this research.

There are several implications for the design of organizational feedback systems that can be drawn from the results of this study and related research. First, feedback provided must relate to organizationally relevant outcomes. Often, compliance with organizational procedures (which may or may not relate to organizationally relevant outcomes) is seen as a desirable end product. Consequently, feedback systems designed to improve procedural compliance may have little relationship to the attainment of organizational objectives.

Related to this point is the need to carefully define and measure the relationship of identified process behaviors to organizationally relevant outcomes. This problem is especially vivid within public sector human service agencies (Noah, Krapfl, & Maley, 1977) where outcomes seemingly defy empirical definition and the processes related to those outcomes are frequently not clear. This may also help to explain why the focus of change in human service organizations is on process behaviors and not intended outcomes.

Finally, designers of organizational feedback systems should be aware of the possibility that process feedback may reduce innovation which could lead to improved outcome performance. The feedback of a specific process carries the message that the performance of the process is desirable. But, it also implies that the performance of that process behavior is preferable to the performance of other available processes. It is this point that leads Gilbert (1978) to emphasize performance outcomes or accomplishments as opposed to process behaviors. Outcome feedback potentially allows for more innovation and, hence, greater potential improvements in processes intended to achieve those outcomes.

In conclusion, this research has shown that performance feedback and goal setting for staff process behavior is effective in changing that performance in the predicted direction. The relationship of process feedback and outcome feedback on organizationally relevant outcomes is not yet clear.

REFERENCES

Barnes, J. A. (1974). Effects of reality orientation classroom on memory loss, confusion, and disorientation in geriatric patients. *The Gerontologist, 14*, 138-142.

Emmert, G. D. (1978). Measuring the impact of group performance feedback vs. individual performance feedback in an industrial setting. *Journal of Organizational Behavior Management, 1*, 134-141.

Folsom, G. S. (1978). *Teaching materials for reality orientation.* Unpublished manuscript. Available from Reality Orientation Training Program, Veterans Administration Medical Center, Tuscaloosa, Alabama 35404.

Frederiksen, L. W. (1982). The selection of targets for organizational interventions. *Journal of Organizational Behavior Management, 3*, 1-5.

Frederiksen, L. W., and Johnson, R. P. (1981). Organizational behavior management. In M. Hersen, R. M. Eisler, and P. M. Miller (Eds.), *Progress in behavior modification*, Vol 12. New York: Academic Press.

Gilbert, T. F. (1978). *Human competence: Engineering worthy performance*. New York: McGraw-Hill.

Grant, F. E. (1977). *Handbook for facilitators: A comprehensive older person rehabilitation program*. Catawba, Va.: Catawba Hospital.

Harris, C. S., and Ivory, P. B. C. B. (1976). An outcome evaluation of reality orientation therapy with geriatric patients in a state mental hospital. *The Gerontologist, 6*, 16, 496-503.

Harshbarger, D. (1979, June). *Understanding systems and delivering community mental health services*. Paper presented at the fifth annual convention of the Association for Behavior Analysis, Dearborn, Michigan.

Hollander, M. A., Plutchik, R., and Horner, V. (1973). Interaction of patient and attendant reinforcement programs: The "piggyback" effect. *Journal of Consulting and Clinical Psychology, 41*, 43-47.

Ivancic, M. T., Reif, D. H., Iwata, B. A., Faw, G. D., and Page, T. J. (1981). Evaluating a supervision program for developing and maintaining therapeutic staff-resident interactions during institution care routines. *Journal of Applied Behavior Analysis, 14*, 95-107.

Iwata, B. A., Bailey, J. S., Brown, K. M. Foshee, T. J., and Alpern, M. (1976). A performance-based lottery to improve residential care and training by institutional staff. *Journal of Applied Behavior Analysis, 9*, 417-431.

Maher, C. A. (1981). Improving the delivery of special education and related services in public schools. *Journal of Organizational Behavior Management, 3* (1), 29-44.

Noah, J. C., Krapfl, J. E., and Maley, R. F. (1977). *Behavioral systems analysis: An integration of behavior analysis and systems analysis to meet the demands of accountability*. Unpublished manuscript. Available from Psychology Department, West Virginia University, Morgantown, W. Va. 26505.

Pommer, D. A., and Streedbeck, D. (1974). Motivating staff performance in an operant learning program for children. *Journal of Applied Behavior Analysis, 7*, 217-221.

Pommerleau, O. F., Bobrove, P. H., and Smith, R. H. (1973). Rewarding psychiatric aides for the behavioral improvement of assigned patients. *Journal of Applied Behavior Analysis, 6*, 383-409.

Application of a Personalized System of Instruction to a Large, Personnel Training Program

John E. Ford

ABSTRACT. Despite the overwhelming success of Personalized Systems of Instruction (PSI) in academic and organizational settings, there continues to be unfounded criticism and resistance to its application in personnel training programs.
Further, no study has been conducted to empirically evaluate its application in the health care setting. The present study examined the application of a "pure" PSI to a large health care personnel training program. Effectiveness, efficiency and cost factors were analyzed. Results indicated the superiority of the PSI approach compared to the traditional, group lecture method. Results were compared to previous investigations, and future directions for research in the organizational setting were discussed.

Personalized Systems of Instruction (PSI) are approaches to teaching and learning based on developments in Psychology and related fields over the past 20 years. More specifically, Keller (1968) identified the basic elements of "pure" PSI, which include: mastery of material; individualized learning rates (self-pacing); presentation of small, sequential units of information; well-defined behavioral objectives for each unit of information; objective performance evaluation with immediate feedback; and one-to-one interaction between instructors and students. The PSI format requires the learner to meet predetermined criteria for, or "master" each unit of information. To master information, the learner is permitted to repeat learning exercises, repeat evaluations of performance, receive immediate performance feedback, and consult with the instructor as needed. Each learner proceeds through the units of information at a pace amenable to his or her own learning rate, and

57

which takes into account other demands on the learner's time. *Behavioral Instruction: An Evaluative Review* (Johnson and Ruskin, 1977) provides a comprehensive examination of the essential elements of PSI.

Fifteen years of research with PSI in the academic setting has been reviewed by Hursh (1976), Johnson and Ruskin (1977), and others (Kulik, 1976; Robin, 1976). This body of research provides convincing evidence that the approach is more effective, more efficient, and results in greater retention of information over time, than conventional approaches to instruction.

In the organizational setting, personnel training approaches employing the basic elements of PSI have often been referred to as Programmed Instruction, but the results of their application have been consistent with findings in the academic setting. In a comprehensive review of PSI applications in Great Britain, Shirley-Smith (1968) reported reduced training time and improved performance in personnel training programs for telephone operators, salespersons, machine operators, and trade apprentices. In a similar review, Mayo (1969) described the use of PSI in the U.S. Navy's Air Technical Training program. In addition to discussing variations in techniques, the role of instructors, and consumer acceptance, Mayo reported that the PSI approach was at least as effective and less costly than the more traditional classroom program. PSI has also been applied successfully in training Civil Defense Coordinators (Ruskjer, 1971), in a vocationally-oriented Adult Basic Training program (Waite, 1971), in a Bell Systems technical training program for mid-managers (Kotch, 1973), in a retraining program for Dow Chemical Company sales personnel (Steffens, 1974), and in a new pilot training program for United Airlines (Cain, 1980).

Despite the empirically-demonstrated superiority of PSI in the academic setting, and its successful application in the organizational setting, the approach continues to be viewed with reservation by managers of personnel training programs. Smith (1980) summarized this view in a recent article, where he contended that PSI and traditional instruction have their place in personnel training programs, but that neither is inherently superior.

As a demonstration project, the present study examined the application of a "pure" PSI approach to a large personnel training program in a health care facility. Curriculum development, trainee performance, cost and efficiency factors were considered and discussed.

METHOD

Participant and Training Course Description

The study was conducted in a large, residential facility for mentally retarded persons, that employed approximately 1750 staff. Of these 1750 positions, approximately 750 were health care technicians. The health care technician positions required the completion of a facility-managed training course for entry. The health care training course was divided into four modules, including: Basic Care; Preventive Intervention Techniques; First Aid; and Advanced Care and Habilitation. Each module was further divided into units, ranging from as few as four units per module to as many as 16 units per module. A comprehensive performance evaluation was required for each module that included both written test questions, and practice that involved demonstration of skills, which were assessed using behavioral rating checklists. It was the policy of the facility that a trainee score a minimum of 80% on each module before entering a regular health care position. Further, a trainee was permitted, by policy, to repeat a module once if the 80% criterion was not achieved. Failure to achieve a score of 80% on one or more modules after two attempts resulted in dismissal.

Thirty health care technician trainees were selected by random draw to participate in the study from a group of 54 newly hired trainees.

Design

A quasi-experimental randomized design, described by Bruning and Kintz (1977), was used to assess the PSI approach to health care training, compared to traditional training techniques. The health care trainees selected for the study were matched according to age, sex, education, and previous experience, and randomly assigned to either a control or an experimental group. The experimental group completed the training course using the PSI approach, while the control group followed the traditional method of instruction. Because of the field study nature of the investigation, and because the control group and experimental group were roughly equivalent in terms of age, sex, education and experience, no pretest was administered for matching participants and assigning them to groups. Trainees assigned to the control group had a mean age of 22.5

years, averaged 3.2 months of previous experience, and had graduated from high school. Experimental group trainees had a mean age of 22.2 years, averaged 3.0 months of previous experience, and had graduated from high school. Nine matched participant pairs were females, while the remaining six pairs were males.

Procedure

Experimental group. All trainees in the experimental group completed the training course using a personalized system of instruction. A behavioral objective and an 80% mastery criterion were established for each unit within each module. All course activities occurred in a Training Center, which was established specifically for the PSI. Study guides, videotapes of pertinent information and demonstrations, and performance evaluation materials were available at the Training Center. In addition, at least two Training Specialists were available at all times at the Training Center to check training materials in and out, administer performance evaluations, provide immediate performance feedback, and provide clarifications and answers to trainees' questions on a one-to-one basis.

Experimental group trainees were required to complete an orientation unit that ensured their understanding of the PSI approach and of what was expected of them. Trainees were permitted to move through the units, sequentially, at their own pace, and could work on units from different modules simultaneously. It should be noted, however, that completion of the Basic Care module was a prerequisite for working on units from the Advanced Care and Habilitation module. Trainees were permitted to repeat the performance evaluation for any unit as many times as necessary until the 80% mastery criterion was achieved. Practice effects were controlled for by testing on multiple, equivalent forms of individual unit evaluations. Following the completion of all the units for a given module, trainees were required to take the comprehensive performance evaluation for the module, according to facility policy.

Control group. All trainees in the control group completed the training course using traditional teaching and training methods. Trainees met in a classroom from 8:00 a.m. to 5:00 p.m. each work day. A Training Specialist led the class, presented lectures, showed videotapes and films, and conducted demonstrations. The group worked on one module at a time, and moved through the information at a pace determined by the Training Specialist. When the Training Specialist completed training for a given module, control group trainees were required to take the comprehensive performance evaluation for the module, according to facility policy. No unit evaluations were given. Control group trainees were permitted to schedule individual time with the Training Specialist to discuss problems, and receive tutoring.

With the exception of the PSI Orientation unit, which the Control Group did not receive, participants in both the Experimental Group and Control Group used the same study guides, observed the same demonstrations and videotape recordings, and, in general, experienced the same course content. The only difference between the two groups was the method of instruction.

Dependent measures. To assess *effectiveness* of training approaches, mean performance across the comprehensive evaluations for the four modules was recorded and compared. In addition, the facility's standard work performance appraisal instrument was used to compare actual on-the-job performance of the participants. The trainee's immediate supervisor conducted the performance appraisal 90 days following the completion of the direct care training program, which was required by facility policy. Supervisors were not informed of the study, or that some of their health care staff had been trained using the PSI approach. Though no formal tests for reliability and validity have been conducted, the performance appraisal instrument had been used by health care supervisors for over two years prior to the study in assessing health care technician work performance.

Efficiency. Efficiency was measured by recording the number of hours each trainee spent in training. Experimental group members logged the times of their entry to and exit from the Training Center. The Training Specialist in charge of the control group recorded the length of each class day and noted if any control group trainees were absent from class. In addition, the control group Training Specialist recorded the amount of time each trainee spent in completing the module performance evaluations, and noted the duration of any special tutoring occurring outside the classroom situation.

A second measure of efficiency was the course completion rate. Since the penalty for not completing the course was dismissal, low completion rates represented a substantial loss for the facility. When a trainee failed to complete the course and was dismissed, no return was realized on the investment of the trainee's salary, and the Training Specialist's time and effort.

Training costs. Training costs for both groups were assessed in a similar manner. For the experimental group the startup costs for the Training Center and the Training Specialist costs were summed, then this amount was divided equally among group trainees. This "fixed" cost was then added to the trainee time cost, which was obtained by multiplying the number of hours in training by the trainee's hourly rate of pay. The control group's training costs were calculated in the same manner, except no startup costs were included. In that course materials were developed prior to the study and were equivalent for both groups, these costs were not included.

RESULTS

Findings for each measure taken on the PSI group and the Traditional Method group are summarized in Table 1. For these measures of effectiveness, a t-test for related measures, described by Bruning and Kintz (1977), was used to compare module performance evaluation scores for the two groups. The PSI group aver-

Table 1

Summary of Findings

Measure	PSI Method	Traditional Method
Effectiveness Measures		
Mean Module Performance Evaluation Score	94.20%	83.93%
Mean Job Performance Evaluation Score	81.60%	75.85%
Efficiency Measures		
Mean Training Time Per Participant	47.32 hrs	165.30 hr.
Percent of Group Completing Training Course	100%	73%
Cost Measures		
Mean Training Cost Per Participant	$236.60	$833.36
Total Training Cost	$3,549.00	$12,500.40

aged 94.20% correct on the module evaluations, which was significantly higher (t=2.96, df=14, p < .01) than the 83.93% average for the Traditional Method group. Similarly, the PSI group's mean rating on the facility's standard job performance evaluation was 81.60%, which included those who scored below 80%. This mean rating was significantly higher (F=15.71, df=1,25, p < .01) than that of the Traditional Method group, which averaged 75.85%. An analysis of variance technique, also described by Bruning and Kintz (1977), was used to analyze job evaluation scores in that these data were collected 90 days following the training program, and, at that time, the number of participants in the two groups was no longer even, due to dismissals.

Efficiency measures included training time per participant and training course completion rates. A t-test for related measures was used for comparisons on the first measure, while a test for significance of difference between two proportions was used for the latter measure. The PSI group completed the course in significantly less time (t=3.47, df=14, p < .01) compared to the Traditional Method group. The mean training time per PSI group participant was 47.32 hours relative to 165.30 hours for the Traditional Method group. Only 11 of the 15 Traditional Method group participants, or 73%, completed the training course according to policy. All PSI group trainees, or 100%, completed the course which was a significantly greater proportion (z=2.45, p < .05), comparably.

The cost of training per PSI group participant was $236.00, which was significantly less expensive (t=4.14, df=14, p < .001) relative to the $833.36 cost per Traditional Method participant. Total cost for the PSI group and Traditional Method group was $3549.00 and $12,500.40, respectively. As noted above, only 11 of the 15 Traditional Method trainees completed the course according to policy. The four who did not complete were unable to score 80% on the module performance evaluations after two attempts, and were dismissed or demoted. The failure of these four to enter into Direct Care positions represented a $3,333.44 loss in training costs.

DISCUSSION

Results of the present investigation demonstrate the overwhelming superiority of the PSI approach, compared to the traditional group lecture method, as applied to the large personnel training program described here. PSI trainees scored higher on a comprehensive evaluation and were rated as more skillful workers by their supervisors, which is consistent with research cited by Shirley-Smith (1968), Mayo's (1969) broad study of programmed instruction with Naval personnel, and Cain's (1980) application of PSI to the new pilot orientation program at United Airlines. In addition, PSI trainees completed the training program more quickly and, as a group, had a substantially higher course completion rate than their counterparts in the traditional training method group. These findings are consistent with studies by Waite (1971), Kotch and Lampkin (1973) and Cain (1980), which also reported reduced training time and higher completion rates. In sum, the PSI approach produced better prepared employees at a greatly reduced cost.

This study indicates, as do the vast majority of other investigations of PSI in both organizational and academic settings, that it is the training method of choice. However, criticisms and a general reluctance to use PSI persist.

One criticism of PSI has centered around the speculation that the technology can only be applied to teaching simple, academically oriented skills. The majority of skills taught in the health care program decribed here were neither academically-oriented, nor simple. This result lends support to Semb's view (Semb, 1976; Semb and Spencer, 1976) that complex skills, whether they are academically-oriented or job related, are not inherent to any particular instructional method. Instead, they are a function of the goals that an instructor or training manager sets.

A second criticism of PSI, that Smith (1980) feels is especially relevant to the organizational/industrial setting, is that it is boring and monotonous for trainees, and reduces instructors to clerks. If the goal of staff training departments or programs is to produce the best trained and most skilled employee, as efficiently as possible, then this research suggests that PSI is the method of choice. If, instead, the goal is to provide an entertaining diversion for trainees and instructors, perhaps the conventional, lecture method should be selected. As Dressler (1971) has pointed out, the lecture is as much a theatrical performance as a learning exercise.

Clearly, a substantial number of studies must be conducted to support the total application of PSI to all staff training programs in the health care setting. This study demonstrates PSI's short-term effectiveness with a large, stable training program. Research in progress should answer questions concerning retention of skills over time. Analysis of PSI's effectiveness as target populations increase or decrease in size or similarity must be conducted. Cost-benefit analyses of PSI, as the life expectancies of course information or courses, themselves, decrease, should be completed. Studies of course management factors should answer questions concerning a given organization's ability to operate a successful PSI program. Though these and other questions need to be answered empirically, PSI appears to have a great deal to offer organizations that are interested in effective, efficient and less expensive personnel training programs.

REFERENCES

Bruning, J. L., & Kintz, B. L. (1977). *Computational handbook of statistics.* Scott, Foresman, and Company, Glenview, Ill.

Cain, D. J. (1980). New hire pilot training at United Airlines. *NSPI Journal, 14*(2), 9-10.

Dressler, A. J. 1971. Teaching without lectures. *Rice University Review, 6,* 9-12.

Hursh, D. E. (1976). Personalized systems of instruction: What do the data indicate? *Journal of Personalized Instruction, 1,* 91-105.

Johnson, K. R., & Ruskin, R. S. 1977. *Behavioral instruction: An evaluative review.* American Psychological Association, Washington, D.C.

Keller, F. S. (1968). "Goodbye, teacher..." *Journal of Applied Behavior Analysis, 1,* 79-89.

Kotch, R. A., & Lampkin, P. F. (1973). The administration of individualized instruction for middle managers. *NSPI Newsletter, 12*(7), 1-4.

Kulik, J. A., 1976. PSI: A formative evaluation. In B. A. Green (Ed.), *Personalized instruction in higher education: Proceedings of the second national conference.* Washington, D.C.: Center for Personalized Instruction, Georgetown University.

Mayo, G. D. (June, 1969). Programmed instruction in technical training. Bureau of Naval Personnel (Research Report 69-28).

Robin, A. L. (1976). Behavioral instruction in the college classroom: A review. *Review of Educational Research, 46,* 313-354.

Ruskjer, N. L. (1971). Programmed orientation to a complex position. *NSPI Journal, 10*(7), 11-14.

Semb, G. (1976). An experimental analysis of personalized instruction: A case study from the Land of Oz. In B. A. Green (Ed.), *Personalized instruction in higher education: Proceedings of the second national conference.* Washington, D.C.: Center for Personalized Instruction, Georgetown University.

Semb, G., & Spencer, R. (1976). Beyond the level of recall: An analysis of complex educational tasks in college and university instruction. In L. E. Fraley and E. A. Vargas (Eds.), *Behavior research and technology in higher education.* Gainesville: University of Florida.

Shirley-Smith, K. (1968). *Programmed learning in integrated industrial training.* London: Gower Press.

Smith, M. E. (1980). Self-paced or leader-led instruction? *Training and Development Journal, 2,* 14-18.

Steffens, H. W. (1974). The development of a programmed learning course for salesmen of "chlorothene" vg solvent. *NSPI Newsletter, 13*(1), 1-9.

Waite, N. (1971). Individualized prescribed instruction in an adult basic education program. *NSPI Journal, 10*(4), 16-18.

Section III:

APPLICATIONS

Description and Evaluation of an Approach to Implementing Programs in Organizational Settings

Charles A. Maher

ABSTRACT. A broad-based approach to implementing programs is described and evaluation information is reported from two investigations of its use by program managers in educational organizations. The approach consists of a framework of program implementation factors from which implementation procedures are derived. The procedures then are used by a manager to help facilitate implementation of a program according to plan. In the first investigation, three program managers were trained in the approach to assist them in implementing a behavioral group counseling program in three public high schools. In the second investigation, a program manager was trained to help implement a case management system in an elementary school. Results of both investigations suggest that managers were able to utilize the program implementation procedures, with their respective programs being more completely implemented when the procedures were applied. Reactions about the approach obtained from human service program managers, following both investigations, suggest that it may be a worthwhile managerial strategy. Advantages and limitations of the approach are considered and its relationship to organizational behavior management is discussed.

Implementing programs in organizational settings is a complex and challenging task for most managers (Prue & Frederiksen, 1982). Increased recognition exists among program managers that they must become more adept at assuring that programs for which they have responsibility are implemented as designed (Hauser, 1982; Leithwood & Montgomery, 1980). Managerial concern about implementation is apparent with respect to a range of programs in diverse organizational settings, including academic and vocational programs in public schools and colleges, counseling and psychotherapy in community mental health centers, training efforts in business, and administrative procedures such as client case management systems in rehabilitation facilities.

Implementing programs in organizational settings has become a priority area of managerial concern for several reasons. First, there is growing awareness that implementation is not a straightforward, linear task, attended to by a manager only when a program begins. Increasingly, managers have begun to appreciate that, in order to increase the likelihood that a program will occur as planned, attention to implementation is necessary at the time of program design (Gibson, Ivancevich, & Donnelly, 1979). A second reason for concern about implementation reflects the need for managers to document delivery of their programs as a means of being accountable to executive boards for use of program funds (Wholey, 1980). A third reason has to do with recent guidelines for program planning and evaluation which suggests that, in order to develop and improve public programs, attention needs to focus on facilitating and evaluating program implementation (Cronbach, 1982; Joint Committee, 1981).

Recent theory, research, and opinion in areas of organizational change and management also support the need for an increased focus on program implementation as well as the development of program implementation strategies. Contemporary thought in these areas further suggests that a broad-based view—an organizational systems perspective—can be a useful one for managers to take in implementing programs. From such a vantage point, a range of factors and forces operating on and within an organization must be identified and taken into account when attempting program implementation. For example, Weiss and Bucuvalas (1977), based upon investigations in social service organizations, have concluded that staff awareness of and commitment toward program purpose and goals are important determinants of program operation. Berman and McLaughlin (1978) and Glasser and Backer (1980), drawing upon data obtained from implementation of educational and mental health programs, assert that staff involvement in the implementation process is critical to a program's remaining in operation after implementation. Davis and Salasin (1975) and literature synthesized by the Human Interaction Research Institute (1976) have emphasized the importance of gathering information about the readiness of an organization to implement a new program as a basis for deciding how to proceed with implementation efforts. Miller (1978) and Maher (1981) have demonstrated how systematic reinforcement of staff for performing assigned program roles and functions can enhance efficiency of program functioning. Janis and Mann (1977) and Katz and Kahn (1978) have discussed the need for explicit program policies and procedures to assure that staff can successfully implement a program. Prue and Frederiksen (1982) and Bonoma (1977) have considered the issue of resistance to program change and have highlighted the need for managers to systematically incorporate a range of implementation strategies to overcome staff resistance to new approaches. Fullan and Pomfret (1977), in an extensive review of implementation of curricular and instructional programs in public schools, concluded that strategies for program implementation must intergrate a range of organizational domains, and that managers must be trained in systematic approaches to implementation. Cronbach (1982), Kratochwill and Bergan (1978), Leithwood and Montgomery (1980), Patton (1978), Hauser (1982), and Maher and Bennett (in press) have illustrated the importance of evaluating program implementation as a basis for improving program operation.

To date, theory, research, and opinion about program implementation in organizational settings has been valuable in several ways: (1) awareness of the need to take a broad-based view of the task has been increased, (2) factors that influence implementation have been identified, (3) guidelines for implementing programs have been defined. However, descriptions of practical approaches for implementing programs in organizational settings have been virtually non-existent, and data supporting potentially effective approaches have not been reported. A practical approach to program implementation is one that provides a framework and set of procedures for effectively guiding managers to implement the program as designed.

In this paper, a particular approach to program implementation is described and results of an evaluation of its use by program managers in various educational organizations are reported. The approach was derived from the theory, research, and opinion discussed above as well as from the author's fifteen years of employment as an administrator in school and university settings and his experience as a managerial consultant to public agencies. The approach can be considered to be a broad-based, organizational behavior management strategy, one that has been applied by the author and colleagues with numerous kinds of programs. In the first part of the paper, the factors that provide a framework for the approach and the program implementation procedures derived from these factors are described. Evaluation results then are reported of two formative investigations in which this approach was used by managers to facilitate implementation of two kinds of programs: (a) a group counseling program for conduct problem adolescents in public high schools; and (b) a system for managing individualized educational programs (IEPs) of handicapped students in an elementary school. Results of reactions of human service managers to the approach also are reported, and advantages and limitations of the strategy are discussed.

DESCRIPTION OF THE APPROACH

In this section, factors that provide a framework for the approach are delineated. Then, a description of the program implementation procedures derived from the factors is provided.

Program Implementation Factors

The framework reflects seven factors that are seen as being important for a manager to consider when attempting to facilitate program implementation. These seven factors can be remembered by the acronym, DURABLE: *D*iscussing, *U*nderstanding, *R*einforcing, *A*cquiring, *B*uilding, *L*earning, and *E*valuating. These factors reveal a range of planning and evaluation activities that suggest how a manager may proceed with implementation. Consideration of the seven factors highlights the importance of active staff involvement in program implementation. Such involvement is seen as helping to create a sense of staff ownership of the program being implemented.

Discussing. This factor focuses on the time prior to program implementation. It suggests that a manager meet with relevant individuals or groups to discuss important aspects of the program. At those meetings, information discussed with staff includes: (a) purpose, goals, and objectives of the program to be implemented; (b) nature and scope of the activities that are to be employed by staff; (c) implementation timelines, dates, and responsibilities; and (d) procedures for staff supervision. At the meetings, the manager encourages staff to identify aspects of the program that are not clear to them and to discuss issues of concern (e.g., contractual issues, work load).

Understanding. This factor also involves the time period prior to implementation. It reflects managerial activities designed to clarify the extent to which the organization is ready to implement the program. Information about organizational readiness can be helpful in design and in suggesting areas where additional staff discussion, program development, etc., may be indicated. The AVICTORY strategy (Davis & Salasin, 1975) is a way of obtaining readiness information. Using this strategy, information can be obtained by a manager on 8 dimensions: *A*bility, *V*alues, *I*dea, *C*ircumstances, *T*iming, *O*bligation, *R*esistance, *Y*ield. Information about these dimensions can be gathered by means of structured interviews or questionnaires conducted with staff and other audiences, such as executive board members, affected by implementation (Maher & Bennett, in press). Examples of questions that can be used by a manager in gathering organizational readiness information about a program to be implemented are:

Ability

- Do staff possess skills and knowledge prerequisite to successful program implementation?
- Are necessary resources (e.g., budget, facilities) available to implement the program?

Values

- Is the program consonant with the prevailing philosophy and goals of the organization?
- Is the program consonant with the professional values of staff and others (e.g., board members)?

Idea

- Is it clear to staff and others as to the nature and scope of the program?
- Is the idea behind the program "tryable" and of potential usefulness?

Circumstances

- Does the present leadership and administrative situation in the organization appear to be conducive to implementation of the program?

Timing

- Is this the appropriate time to implement the program or expand it to other sites?

Obligation

- Is the need for the program apparent to staff, administrators, and community?

Resistance

- To what extent will individuals or groups resist implementation?

Yield

- Are the expected positive consequences of the program apparent to staff?

Information gathered in response to these kind of questions allows judgments to be made about how to further develop a program (e.g., additional staff training, further discussion with key people), as well as when to implement it (e.g., delay implementation to next calendar year).

Reinforcing. This factor reflects efforts of a manager to reinforce staff for carrying out their program implementation roles and responsibilities. Toward this end, a range of reinforcers may be used by the manager, particularly those involving (a) on-site verbal praise of staff; (b) written memos or notes to staff or supervisors expressing appreciation of and recognition for engaging in prescribed activities; (c) public posting of relevant implementation data (e.g., percent of sessions held, participant attendance rates); and (d) social reinforcement and encouragement for active participation of staff in evaluating program implementation and outcome.

Acquiring. In order for a program to operate relative to how it was designed, certain pre-conditions may need to exist in the organization. This factor suggests that a manager must make certain that important program pre-conditions are "acquired" such as (a) ensuring that program purpose, goals, and objectives have been clearly written and communicated to others; (b) providing necessary pre-program training to implementers; (c) seeing to it that materials and equipment have been ordered, and facilities renovated; and (d) obtaining sanctions of policies, procedures, or budget essential for program operation.

Building. This factor serves to emphasize that a manager build (develop) cooperative working relationships with planners and implementers. Toward that end, positive expectations about the program are displayed by the manager, administrative assistants, and supervisors during all meetings with staff. Active involvement of the manager with staff in matters of program design and implementation can be a way of (a) fostering positive expectations about the program or system; and (b) clarifying positive manager-staff implementation relationships.

Learning. This factor reflects managerial activities designed to help implementers improve their ability to carry out their implementation roles and responsibilities. Learning of this nature occurs within a supervisory context where a manager, often with the help of coordinators and supervisors, seeks to systematically identify staff who need to become (a) more knowledgeable about some aspect of their implementation functions; (b) more skillful in performing certain functions; and/or (c) more aware of the importance of their role in relation to those of other staff. If knowledge, skills, or affective needs are identified, then information dissemination or training activities designed to promote learning can occur. Once a program implementer has achieved an acceptable level of performance, verbal or written performance feedback can be used to assist in maintaining the desired level.

Evaluating. This factor reflects the management activity of evaluating the extent of program implementation, and the degree of program outcome success. Implementation evaluation can focus on several questions: (1) Did the appropriate target group receive the program?; (2) Did staff perform the required activities as expected?; (3) Were prescribed methods and materials utilized?; (4) What changes were made in program design following implementation?; (5) What differences existed in program operation across sites. Methods used to gather information in response to these questions may include staff interview and survey procedures, on-site observation, and permanent product review (see Maher & Bennett, in press, for specific examples of approaches to implementation evaluation). Outcome evaluation activities address specific questions such as: (1) To what extent were program goals attained?; (2) How did consumers react to the program?; (3) Were any side-effects observed? (4) Was the program a worthwhile investment?

Program Implementation Procedures

Based on the seven DURABLE factors as well as managerial activities suggested by each factor, program implementation procedures can be derived. These procedures are the ones that are used by a manager to help facilitate implementation of a program. The procedures are applied by a manager in a particular sequence. Fourteen procedures constitute the approach. These procedures are listed below, with the corresponding DURABLE factor seen in parentheses:

1. Gather information about the extent to which the organization is ready to undertake implementation of the program. Information is gathered on the 8 AVICTORY dimensions by means of interview, permanent product review, questionnaire, and observational methods. (*U*nderstanding)
2. Analyze and report the readiness information obtained, and involve key individuals and groups in considering what modifications may be needed in program design, prior to program implementation. (*U*nderstanding)
3. Describe the program to be implemented in a written form that is meaningful to program implementers and provide them with copies of the written documentation. (*B*uilding)
4. Conduct meetings with individuals and groups who will implement the program so as to involve them in discussing:
   a. program purpose, goals, and objectives
   b. nature and scope of program activities
   c. implementation timelines, dates, and repsonsibilities
   d. nature and scope of supervisory relationships
   e. contractual and procedural issues and concerns. (*D*iscussing)
5. Disseminate public relations information about the program to key professionals and community members. (*B*uilding)
6. Provide necessary staff training, prior to program implementation. (*A*cquiring)
7. Obtain sanctions for the program to operate; order needed equipment and materials; renovate facilities. (*A*cquiring)

8. Reinforce implementers for performing their prescribed roles and functions by means of:
   a. written letters or memos to supervisors
   b. performance feedback data. (*R*einforcing)
9. Appraise performance of implementers as they deliver the program to determine if additional training is indicated or if additional information about their roles and functions is required. (*L*earning)
10. Provide additional training or information to program implementers. (*L*earning)
11. Reinforce implementers for improved performance, following provision of additional training or information. (*R*einforcing)
12. Evaluate extent to which the program has been implemented in terms of:
    a. targets who received the program
    b. methods and materials employed by implementers
    c. facilities utilized. (*E*valuating)
13. Evaluate extent to which program outcomes have occurred in terms of:
    a. goal attainment
    b. consumer reaction
    c. side-effects. (*E*valuating)
14. Revise the program as required. (*E*valuating)

In the next two sections of the paper, two investigations are presented to provide evaluation information about the effectiveness of this approach to program implementation.

INVESTIGATION 1: IMPLEMENTING A BEHAVIORAL GROUP COUNSELING PROGRAM

Description of the Program to Be Implemented

The program to be implemented was a behavioral group counseling program, previously reported as effective with conduct disordered adolescents (Maher, 1981; Maher & Barbrack, 1982; Maher & Barbrack, in press). The program's target population was high school students manifesting school adjustment problems (e.g., truancy, absenteeism, alcohol abuse, fighting with peers, refusal to complete class and homework assignments). The program's purpose was to improve adjustment of program participants by assisting them to develop positive, school-related social and academic behaviors. Each program that was implemented involved between 6-8 pupils who met with a state certified school counselor for 10 weekly group counseling sessions. The program was structured by five counseling phases that occurred sequentially over the 10 sessions. Activities of each phase were centered around a particular question. The five phases and related questions were: (1) Problem Identification (What is my problem with respect to succeeding at school)?. (2) Plan Development (What is my plan for solving my problem?). (3) Plan Implementation (Am I following through on my plan?). (4) Plan Evaluation (Is my plan working?). (5) Plan Revision (Should my plan be revised)? During the group counseling program, it was expected that each pupil develop, implement, and evaluate an individualized self-improvement plan, based on discussions with the counselor and other pupils in the group.

Organizational Settings

One high school in each of three New Jersey urban public school districts comprised the three settings for the investigation. The three high schools, termed School X, School Y, and School Z for the investigation, were similar on various organizational characteristics: (1) Pupil population (X = 1,600 pupils; Y = 1,700 pupils; Z = 1,550 pupils). (2) Grade level structure (9-12 in all schools). (3) Number of full-time counseling staff (School X = 6 counselors; School Y = 6 counselors; School Z = 5 counselors). (4) Similar kinds of counseling and guidance activities provided students.

In each setting, it was the intent of the school district's director of pupil personnel services and the high school counseling staff to implement the 10 week group counseling program, as designed, for selected groups of students, continuously throughout the school year. Since each high school's academic year was organized in terms of four, 10 week grading periods, it was possible to employ a multiple baseline across schools design for the investigation. For the investigation, baseline was considered as the grading period(s) before the program manager (director of pupil personnel services) was trained and engaged in the approach to program implementation described above. The grading periods following managerial training were used to assess possible effects of such training on extent of group counseling program implementation.

Program Managers and Managerial Training

Program managers were the directors of pupil personnel services of each school district. These individuals had overall responsibility for ensuring that the group counseling program was implemented as designed in the respective high schools, with different groups of pupils, continuously throughout the school year. The three managers all possessed master's degrees in school administration, previous experiences as school counselors or psychologists, and all had been functioning in their current positions for several years. Each manager was unaware of the existence of each other; all were debriefed following the investigation.

During baseline, each manager participated in a three-day workshop, but not at the same workshop as the other two managers. The workshop was provided by a school psychologist, at a centrally located site. Workshop activities consisted of didactic presentations, simulation exercises, and case examples organized by means of two training modules: (1) "An Organizational Overview of Enhancing Program Implementation." (2) "DURABLE Factors and Program Implementation Procedures." At the workshop, the managers received training in the specific program implementation procedures seen in Table 1.

TABLE 1

Implementation Procedures
for the Group Counseling Program

1. Gather information about the high school's readiness for group counseling by using the AVICTORY questions in interviews with school principals, counselors, and a representative sample of teaching staff.
2. Analyze readiness information obtained by determining areas where readiness is low, and meet with principal, counselors, and teachers in deciding about modifications that need to be made in group counseling program design.

TABLE 1 (continued)

3. Develop a written group counseling program design that describes program purpose, rationale, and activities, and disseminate that information to principal, vice-principal, and teaching staff.
4. Conduct a meeting with all counselors who will implement the group counseling program to discuss program purpose, implementation responsibilities, timelines, supervisory procedures, and related issues (conduct follow-up meetings, if necessary).
5. Disseminate information about the group counseling program in the local newspaper and in parent-teacher organization newsletters, prior to program implementation.
6. Provide counselors with the procedure manual about the group counseling program, and review the phases of the group counseling approach with them at a ''training refresher workshop.''
7. Obtain sanction from the school principal and parents for pupil participation in the group counseling program.
8. Provide verbal reinforcement to counselors for implementing the program according to the phases of the program, at weekly ''implementation meetings.''
9. Identify areas of program implementation where counselors need additional training or information, based on discussions at the implementation meetings.
10. Provide additional training or information during the period of time the group counseling program is being implemented.
11. Provide verbal reinforcement to counselors who have improved their group counseling performance following the additional training or information provision, at individual meetings or contacts.
12. Evaluate the extent to which the specified number of group counseling sessions occurred and how they occurred.
13. Evaluate the extent to which each pupil's counseling goals were attained and how participants reacted to counseling process and counseling outcomes.
14. Revise the group counseling program, based on information gathered from implementation and outcome evaluation.

Implementation Measures, Measurement Reliability, and Results

Three measures were used to assess extent of implementation of the behavioral group counseling program in Schools X, Y, and Z prior to and following training of the managers in the program implementation procedures seen in Table 1. These measures, measurement reliability data, and results obtained on each measure are summarized below.

(1) *Occurrence of group counseling sessions.* This measure reflected the extent to which the 10 group counseling sessions occurred for each program implemented (i.e., each set of 10 week sessions scheduled to be provided to a particular group of pupils). Occurrence of group counseling sessions was expressed as a mean percent of occurrence of sessions for each program implemented in Schools X, Y, and Z, prior to and following managerial training. To arrive at the percent figure, the number of sessions held for each program was compared to the expected number of sessions to be held for that program (n = 10 sessions). Data were obtained on this measure from records kept by each counselor who implemented the program with different groups of pupils throughout the school year.

Figure 1 displays data on the mean percent of occurrence of group counseling sessions conducted in Schools X, Y, and Z prior to and following managerial training. As seen in Figure 1, the mean percent of occurrence of group counseling sessions increased across the three schools only following training (within the time period in which it was anticipated that the procedures would be utilized by the program managers). For School X, it was reported that 18 group counseling programs were scheduled to be implemented pre-training (1st marking period) with the mean percent of occurrence of group counseling sessions for these programs being 54%. However, following training (2nd, 3rd, and 4th marking periods) in School X, although 46 group counseling programs were scheduled to be implemented, the mean percent of occurrence of sessions for these programs rose to 95%. For Schools Y and Z, similar kinds of results were obtained. For School Y, 35 counseling programs were scheduled during pre-training (1st and 2nd marking periods), with a mean percent of occurrence of sessions for these programs being 38%. Following training (3rd and 4th marking periods), 31 programs were scheduled to be implemented, with a mean percent of occurrence for these programs increasing to 90%. For School Z, 39 programs were scheduled prior to training (1st, 2nd, and 3rd mark-

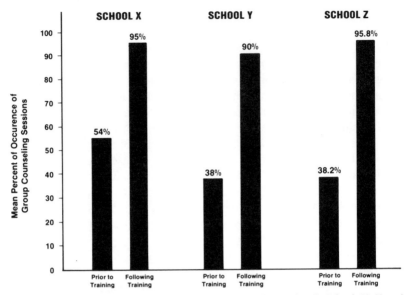

FIGURE 1. Mean percent of occurrence of group counseling sessions in Schools X, Y, and Z prior to and following managerial training. For School X, prior to training (baseline) was the 1st marking period of the school year while following training was the 2nd, 3rd, and 4th periods. For School Y, prior to training (baseline) was the 1st and 2nd periods while following training was the 3rd and 4th periods. For School Z, prior to training (baseline) was the 1st, 2nd, and 3rd periods while following training was the 4th marking period.

ing periods) with mean percentage of occurrence of counseling sessions being 38.2%. Following training (4th marking period), 12 programs were offered, with the mean percent of occurrence of sessions being 95.8%.

(2) *Pupil attendance at group counseling programs.* This measure reflected the extent to which pupils who were scheduled to receive group counseling programs during the year actually received those programs. Pupil attendance data were gathered on pupils scheduled for each program from attendance records kept by the respective group counselors. Mean percent of pupil attendance figures were then calculated for the pre-training and post-training periods in Schools X, Y, and Z.

Figure 2 displays data on the mean percent of pupil attendance at the group counseling programs in Schools X, Y, and Z, prior to and following training. As seen in Figure 2, pupil attendance at group counseling increased in the three school sites only after training. For School X, 109 pupils were reported as being scheduled for group counseling programs prior to training (n = 6.1 per program), with the mean percent of pupil attendance being 71.5%. Post-training in School X, revealed 280 pupils were scheduled for group counseling (n = 6.1 per program), and the mean percent of pupil attendance rose to 93.2%. Similar kinds of pupil attendance results were obtained in Schools Y and Z. For School Y, 207 pupils were scheduled for group counseling prior to training (n = 5.9 per program), with the mean percent of attendance of those pupils being 67.8%. Following training, 189 pupils were to receive group counseling (n = 6.1 per program, and the attendance rate of these pupils increased to 97.1%. For School Z, 237 pupils were to receive group counseling during the pre-training period (n = 6.1 per program), with the level of attendance being 74.3%. Following training, 74 pupils were targeted for the program (n = 6.2 per program), and the mean attendance rate rose to 98.3%.

(3) *Utilization of group counseling program phases.* This measure

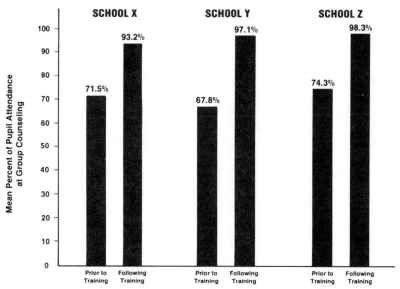

FIGURE 2. Mean percent of pupil attendance at the group counseling programs in Schools X, Y, and Z prior to and following managerial training. For School X, prior to training (baseline) was the 1st marking period of the school year while following training was the 2nd, 3rd, and 4th periods. For School Y, prior to training (baseline) was the 1st and 2nd periods while following training was the 3rd and 4th periods. For School Z, prior to training (baseline) was the 1st, 2nd, and 3rd periods while following training was the 4th marking period.

reflected the extent to which each of the five group counseling program phases were employed by each group counselor for each program implemented. Data were gathered on this measure from counseling program logs kept by the counselors as part of the program. Logs included information about activities of counseling sessions, categorized under the five counseling program phases: (1) Problem Identification. (2) Plan Development. (3) Plan Implementation. (4) Plan Evaluation. (5) Plan Revision. It was expected that during each 10 week counseling program all 5 phases would occur. Two graduate students were used in each school to review the group counseling program logs for these data, and to calculate a mean percent for pre-training and post-training periods. Inter-rater reliability was assessed for each pair of raters by comparing rater agreements divided by rater agreements plus disagreements, multiplied by 100, and then calculating a percent figure. For the two raters in School X, inter-rater reliability was 94.3% for pre-training data, and 96.2% for post-training data. For School Y, inter-rater reliability was 95.1% for pre-training data, and 94.9% for post-training data. For School Z, inter-rater reliability was 97.6% (pre-training) and 98.1% (post-training).

Figure 3 displays the mean percent of group counseling phases utilized per program, across Schools X, Y, and Z, prior to and following training. As seen in Figure 3, there was an increase in counseling phase utilization reported following training. For School X, mean percent of phase utilization was 11.1% during pre-training and 73.9% post-training. For School Y, mean percent of utilization was 20% during pre-training and 83.8% during post-training. For School Z, the pre-training mean percent was 35.8%, while the post-training mean percent was 83.3%.

Utilization of the Procedures by Program Managers

To determine the extent to which Managers X, Y, and Z utilized the program implementation procedures listed in Table 1, a managerial assessment strategy was conducted. Six graduate students in school psychology were hired as assessors. They were instructed by the author in gathering data on implementation of the group counseling program by each manager. Data was collected both prior to and following managerial training in the procedures.

Assessors were trained to employ three data collection methods:

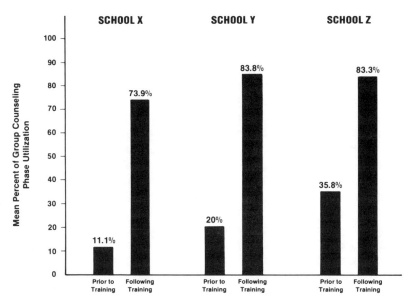

FIGURE 3. Mean percent of group counseling phase utilization in Schools X, Y, and Z prior to and following managerial training. For School X, prior to training (baseline) was the 1st marking period of the school year while following training was the 2nd, 3rd, and 4th periods. For School Y, prior to training (baseline) was the 1st and 2nd periods while following training was the 3rd and 4th periods. For School Z, prior to training (baseline) was the 1st, 2nd, and 3rd periods while following training was the 4th marking period.

(1) interviews of each manager during the school year in order to gather data about procedures 7, 11, 14 (listed in Table 1); (2) review of permanent products generated as a result of procedures 1, 3, 5, 12, 13; and (3) observation of meetings that were part of procedures 2, 4, 6, 8, 9 10. Two assessors were assigned to each high school. Each assessor was requested to employ the three data collection methods and to make two types of ratings: (a) a rating about percent of use of the procedures by each manager prior to and following training, i.e., whether all 14 procedures were so utilized; and (b) a rating about the sequence in which the procedures were used by each manager occurred by a procedure where i.e., whether the procedures occurred in the order specified in Table 1. Based upon the data gathered in the assessment, the author was able to determine reliability of both types of ratings made by the pairs of assessors (raters). Inter-rater reliability of percent of use of the 14 program implementation procedures for each manager, rater agree-

ments regarding use of the procedures were divided by the sum of rater agreements plus disagreements. An agreement was defined as the situation where both assessors indicated that a particular procedure had been used by a manager; a disagreement occurred when one assessor indicated a procedure had been employed, while the other indicated a procedure had not been employed. Using this approach, inter-rater reliability was determined to be the following across the 3 schools for percent of use: School X (pre-training = 100%, post-training = 100%); School Y (pre-training = 97%, post-training = 100%); School Z (pre-training = 97%, post-training = 100%). Ratings of the sequence in which the 14 program implementation procedures were employed by each manager were subjected to a similar approach to inter-rater reliability determination. Assessors had been requested to document the times and dates each procedure was employed by each manager. Consequently, it was possible to determine the extent to which a pair of assessors was in agreement as to the sequence of occurrence of the procedures. In this respect, an agreement was defined as the situation where both assessors indicated that a procedure had occurred at a particular point in the program implementation process. Using this approach, inter-rater reliability was determined to be the following: School X (pre-training = 100%, post-training = 100%); School Y (pre-training = 98%, post-training = 100%); School Z (pre-training = 100%, post-training = 100%).

Results of the managerial assessment strategy conducted in each high school indicated that the program implementation procedures seen in Table 1 were used to a high degree by the three program managers and were consistently employed in the recommended sequence by the managers following training. Managers Y and Z, used 100% of the procedures (14/14) following training while Manager X used 13 of the 14 procedures for a percent of use of 93% (procedure 12 was not employed). Prior to training, though, percent of procedural use was 14% for Manager X (2/14), 14% for Manager Y (2/14), and 21% for Manager Z (3/14). In terms of sequence of occurrence of the procedures, all three managers following training employed all procedures in the order seen in Table 1. These managerial assessment data document that prior to training the three managers employed very few of the program implementation procedures. Following training, the evaluation data suggest that the procedures were employed to a considerable degree as well as consistently used in the recommended order.

Discussion of the Investigation

Results of this investigation should be seen within a formative evaluation context. They suggest the approach may be an effective means of facilitating implementation of group counseling programs in public high schools. Following utilization of the approach by program managers in High Schools X, Y, and Z, marked increases were apparent in occurrence of group counseling sessions, pupil attendance at those sessions, and extent to which group counseling program phases were utilized. Use of a multiple baseline design across schools lends additional credence to the effectiveness of the approach since increases on all measures did not occur in each school until training had taken place. Data derived on program managers' use of the procedures suggest the approach was applied in the three organizational settings. Once the investigation was concluded, the three managers expressed, both to the author and to their respective boards of education, that they were very satisfied with the training they had received in the approach. Furthermore, all three managers indicated that they considered use of the procedures to have been largely responsible for helping them improve the extent to which the group counseling programs were implemented in the schools. Moreover, all managers indicated that they would recommend to the school superintendent that other managers in their organization could benefit from similar training.

INVESTIGATION 2: IMPLEMENTING A CASE MANAGEMENT SYSTEM

Description of the Program to Be Implemented

The program to be implemented was a system for managing the individualized education programs (IEPs) of handicapped children (Maher & Barbrack, 1980). It involved a multidisciplinary case management team of professionals—psychologist, educational consultant, teacher—in gathering a range of information about the IEP of each handicapped child provided with special education services in public schools, pursuant to PL 94-142. This information, gathered throughout the school year on 4 aspects of the IEP of each child, was intended to help the case management team in making IEP development and revision decisions. In using the system, data were to be gathered on 4 aspects of each IEP: (1) IEP design (e.g., appropriateness of goals and objectives). (2) IEP implementation (e.g., frequency of services rendered vs. services planned). (3) IEP goal attainment (e.g., degree of attainment of IEP goals). (4) Consumer reaction to the IEP (e.g., satisfaction of parents). In obtaining this information, team members were to employ a range of techniques: interviews, questionnaires, observations, and review of test data and other products (e.g., student projects). School staff, parents, and children were to serve as data sources, continuously, throughout the school year.

Organizational Settings

An elementary school in each of two New Jersey urban public school districts comprised the settings for the investigation. A coin toss determined the school in which the program implementation procedures were to be utilized by the manager (district director of special education services). School "D" was the designation given to that school; the comparison school was designated as School "N." Based on document reviews and interviews with school principals, both schools previously had been judged similar on various organizational characteristics: (a) pupil ethnic composition; (b) total enrollment; (c) grade-level structure (K-5); (d) number of pupils receiving special education services; (e) size of teaching staff. Furthermore, a multidisciplinary case management team, consisting of a school psychologist, social worker and learning consultant, was employed in each school, two days per week. Each team was responsible for managing the IEPs of handicapped children enrolled in the respective school. Also, each school had a full-time principal and vice-principal, a school-community curriculum council, written school goals and objectives, and a parent teacher organization. Based upon data contained in a board of education report, the principal and vice-principal in each school reported spending between 45-60% of a typical school day in classroom observation and teacher supervision activities. The IEP case management system to be implemented had not previously been used in either school.

Program Managers and Managerial Training

Managers responsible for ensuring that the case management system was implemented in each school were the directors of special education services of each district. Both managers possessed doctoral degrees in special education and several years experience in their positions. Managers were unaware of each other's existence, but were debriefed following the study. Manager D (School D) was provided training in the 14 program implementation procedures seen in Table 2 at a three-day workshop. This workshop, provided to seven other managers from other school districts who were charged with implementing the case management system, was provided by a doctoral-level school psychologist. The workshop occurred at a centrally-located school district, prior to the school year.

In order to provide Manager N with "training attention," but not training in the specific program implementation procedures, that manager participated in a three-day workshop on program planning and evaluation that was provided to school principals and special service directors in a nearby city, by a private consulting firm. It was conducted by a trainer with experience in public school administration and consisted of didactic activities that focused on concepts, principles, and procedures of designing, implementing, and evaluating educational programs in public schools.

TABLE 2

IMPLEMENTATION PROCEDURES FOR THE
CASE MANAGEMENT SYSTEM

1. Gather information about readiness of the elementary school for the case management system by interviewing the principal and members of special and regular education teaching staffs. Information is to be gathered on awareness of these individuals of P.L. 94-142 and the I.E.P. requirement.
2. Analyze readiness information as to areas of readiness in need of improvement, and discuss with principal and staff members at a meeting specifically designated for that purpose.
3. Develop a written description of the case management system that includes information about purpose and activities and relationship of the system to special education law, and disseminate that information to principal, case management team, and school faculty.

TABLE 2 (continued)

4. Conduct meeting with principal and case management team to discuss content of the written description.
5. Disseminate information about the case management system to teaching staff of the school and parents of handicapped children attending the school.
6. Provide training in the four phases of the case management approach to team members, using a training manual (Maher & Barbrack, 1980).
7. Meet with representatives of parents of handicapped children at a formal meeting to explain to them how they can become involved in individualized program design and outcome evaluation relative to their child.
8. Provide written feedback to case management team members on case management performance, on a monthly basis.
9. Identify aspects of case management where team members need additional training or information, once the system is in operation.
10. Provide the additional training or information to specific team members or to entire team.
11. Provide verbal reinforcement to team members or the team as a whole for improved case management performance, following training.
12. Evaluate the extent to which each phase of the case management system has been utilized by the team for each handicapped pupil.
13. Evaluate the extent to which information to be derived from each phase of the program was obtained and provided in a written form to school principal and other audiences.
14. Revise the case management system for the subsequent school year, based on information from implementation and outcome evaluation.

Implementation Measures, Measurement Reliability, and Results

Three measures were used to obtain information about implementation of the IEP case management system in Schools D and N. These measures, measurement reliability data, and results obtained on each measure are summarized below.

(1) *Complete implementation of the IEP case management system.*
This measure reflected the degree to which the case management
system was *completely implemented* in each school. Complete implementation was determined by the extent to which each of the following 4 IEP case management activities occurred for each IEP
during the year: (1) Analysis of IEP design. (2) Evaluation of IEP
implementation. (3) Evaluation of IEP goal attainment. (4) Assessment of consumer reaction to the IEP. Data were gathered on these
activities based on the "Program Evaluation Service Record
(PESR)," a form used in each school upon which team members recorded the dates, times, and persons involved in each of the 4 IEP
case management activities for each IEP provided a handicapped
child.

At the conclusion of the school year, 30 PESRs were randomly
selected from the special service files of each school. Two graduate
students in special education were trained to rate completeness of
implementation of the system in each school, using the above definition of complete implementation. Inter-rater reliability was calculated by comparing number of agreements of each rater about
system completeness divided by rater agreements plus disagreements, multiplied by 100. Inter-rater reliability was 97% for School
D and 94% for School N. In School D, 27 out of 30 of the randomly
selected IEPs were completely implemented (i.e., all 4 activities occurred) for a completion rate of 90%. In School N, 13 out of the 30
randomly selected IEPs were completely implemented for a completion rate of 43.3%.

(2) *Extent of occurrence of IEP case management activities.* This
measure reflected the extent to which the 4 IEP case management
activities occurred for all IEPs developed during the school year.
Extent of activity occurrence was measured by comparing number
of IEPs in which one or more of the 4 activities had occurred relative to total number of IEPs, and then calculating a percentage. In
School D, the total number of IEPs for the year was 78, while the
total number in School N was 85. At the conclusion of the school
year, all PESRs of all handicapped children in both schools were reviewed by two graduate students in special education to determine
extent of use of the 4 activities. Inter-rater reliability was calculated
using the same procedure as described for Measure No. 1 above.
For School D, inter-rater reliability was 96%, while for School N it
was 98%. For the 78 IEPs that were designed or revised during the
year in School D, at least 3 activities had occurred for 73 of them,

and 4 had occurred for 70 of the 73. For the 85 IEPs developed or updated during the year in School N, at least one activity occurred for 54 out of the 85. Of the 54 IEPs, 6 had used one activity; 12 had used two; 14 had used three; and 22 had used all four.

(3) *Durability of the IEP case management system.* This measure reflected the extent to which the IEP case management system was in operation during the school year following the investigation. Data were obtained on this measure by two graduate students in special education. They were asked to rate extent of occurrence of IEP evaluation activities for September through December of the new school year, using the procedures described for Measure No. 2 above. Interrater reliability was 100% in both schools using that procedure. Results revealed large differences between Schools D and N. During the months of September through December, 34 IEPs had been developed or updated in School D. Of those 34 IEPs, all 4 activities had occurred for 30 of them, or 88%. In School N, during the same time period, 26 IEPs had been developed or updated. Of those 26 IEPs, all 4 activities had occurred for only 7 of them, or 26%.

Utilization of the Procedures by Program Managers

To determine the extent to which Manager D utilized the program implementation procedures seen in Table 2, as well as whether Manager N may have employed similar procedures, the managerial assessment strategy described in Investigation No. 1 was employed for the present investigation. Four graduate students in school psychology were hired as assessors. These assessors were instructed by the author to employ three data gathering methods: (1) interview of Manager D to gather data about procedures 1, 9, 11, 14 (see Table 2), and Manager N to gather data about use of similar procedures; (2) review of permanent products generated by Manager D from procedures 3, 5, 8, 12, 13, and similar kinds of products that may have been generated by Manager N; and (3) observation of meetings conducted by Manager D that were part of procedures 2, 4, 6, 7, 10, or similar meetings held by Manager N. Assessors of Manager D were asked to make independent ratings of (a) the percent of use of the 14 procedures by that manager, and (b) the sequence of use of the procedures. Using the approach for determining inter-rater reliability described in Investigation 1, inter-rater reliability was calculated as follows for Manager D: 100% for percent of use; 98% for sequence of use. Assessors of Manager N were asked to describe the procedures employed by that manager. The assessors were then asked to categorize those descriptions under one of the procedures seen in Table 2.

Results of the managerial assessment revealed that Manager D engaged in 100% of the 14 procedures and employed them in the recommended sequence seen in Table 2. Manager N engaged in two activities that could be categorized under procedures 7 and 11. These managerial assessment data can serve to document that Manager D employed the procedures seen in Table 2, while Manager N did not employ the majority of these procedures.

Discussion of the Investigation

Results indicate that the IEP case management system was implemented to a greater degree as well as remained in place for a longer period of time in School D than in School N. Moreover, the procedures were documented as occurring to a greater extent for Manager D, but not Manager N. Given these findings, it seems that the approach may have been an important factor in accounting for differences in case management system implementation between schools. However, given the formative nature of this investigation, it was not possible to rule out factors other than the approach that might explain differences in implementation of the case management system between schools (e.g., prior teacher involvement in monitoring pupil progress, instructional leadership, school climate). Although it was not the intent of the investigation to determine specific procedures that may have been particularly effective, separate discussions following the investigation between the investigator and Manager D and Manager N were somewhat informative. In this regard, Manager D reported that procedures reflected in the factors of discussion and understanding, where staff were actively involved in preparation for implementation, seemed to be the most important elements. In a similar vein, Manager N reported a desire to have spent more time, "up-front," in preparing staff for IEP implementation as well as in discussing with them steps in IEP case management.

REACTIONS OF HUMAN SERVICE MANAGERS

Following both investigations, 9 program managers from different human service organizations were asked to participate in a "potential user reaction procedure." The purpose of the procedure was to obtain reactions from such managers, as potential users of the approach to program implementation described above, about the perceived value of that approach to themselves and other managers. The 9 managers who participated were (a) 3 coordinators of consultation and education from 3 community mental health centers; (b) 3 supervisors of counseling of 3 residential treatment facilities for adolescents; and (c) 3 educational directors of 3 adult day training centers. Six of the reactors possessed doctoral degrees and 3 master's degrees, all in human service-related areas. Reactors were selected randomly from a directory of New Jersey institutions and agencies.

Each human service program manager (reactor) was mailed a packet of materials and asked to engage anonymously in the reaction procedure (confidentiality was assured). These materials were: (1) a description of the 7 DURABLE factors and 14 program implementation procedures; (2) a document explaining the purpose of, and rationale of the approach (i.e., to help managers in assuring a program is implemented as planned); and (3) a "questions sheet," listing 4 questions. Each manager was instructed to review the materials and respond to each question. The first question was: "To what extent would this approach help you implement programs for which you are responsible" (rating scheme: 5 = very great extent; 4 = good extent; 3 = somewhat; 2 = very little; 1 = not at all)? The second question was: "If given an opportunity, would you attend a 3-day workshop on the approach" (rating scheme: 3 = yes; 2 = not certain; 1 = no)? The third question was: "Do you believe the approach would be valuable to other managers who hold similar positions to yours" (rating scheme: same as question 1)? A fourth question asked the manager to list the perceived advantages and drawbacks of the approach. All managers responded to all 4 questions.

Results of this potential user reaction procedure suggested that the 9 human service managers who participated considered the approach to be potentially useful to themselves as well as to other managers. In response to question 1, 7 managers provided a rating of "5"; 1 manager a rating of "3"; and 1 manager a rating of "2." In response to question 2, 6 managers indicated they would attend a 3 day training program; 2 were not sure, and 1 said no. In response to question 3, 8 of the 9 managers indicated that the approach would be valuable to other managers and provided a "5" rating; 1 manager provided a rating of "2." On the open-ended question, most frequently occurring responses about advantages of the approach were: (1) Importance of the delineation of specific procedures (n = 7); (2) Importance of the ordering of the procedures (n = 6); (3) Value of the DURABLE acronym as a way of remembering important program implementation variables (n = 8). In terms of drawbacks, the most frequent response had to do with respondents' concern that some staff may view their involvement in aspects of the approach (e.g., meetings, interviews) as too rigid, as inflexible, or time consuming.

Overall, results of the potential user reaction procedure described above seem to indicate that human service managers may consider the approach to be a potentially valuable one for use in their professional roles. In this regard, 6 of 9 managers indicated that they would receive training in the approach, if provided an opportunity to do so.

GENERAL DISCUSSION

Results of the two investigations suggest the approach to program implementation described above to be a potentially worthwhile, broad-based organizational behavior management strategy for ensuring that programs are implemented and remain in operation. Large increases were observed relative to all implementation measures following utilization of the approach by program managers when introduced sequentially in three organizations. (Investigation 1) and when two organizations were compared (Investigation 2). Assessment of managerial use of the implementation procedures indicated that the procedures were employed by the trained managers in both investigations. Furthermore, the three managers responsible for implementation of the group counseling programs, as well as the manager who used the approach to facilitate IEP case management systems implementation, expressed satisfaction with the training they had received in the strategy. Also informal discussions by the author with all managers in both investigations indicated that they attributed increases in degree of program implementation following training in large part to their utilization of DURABLE activities.

Although it is possible to speculate that the approach is a seemingly effective means of facilitating program implementation, definitive conclusions are not possible, given the design and purpose of the investigations reported above. The two investigations should be considered as formative evaluations of an overall organizational intervention package. It was not the intent of either investigation to determine the specific procedural elements that might be critical components. Results of the two investigations do indicate, however, that additional research seems warranted with managers in human service organizations. Toward this end, investigations such as the ones reported above could occur in school and other human service settings, focusing on the task of enhancing implementation of similar direct client service programs (e.g., counseling programs) as well as case management systems. Additional investigations of this nature can be considered an important next step, since it is possible that situational variables, unique to the current sites but not considered in the investigations, may have been responsible for improved degree of implementation.

The approach described above possesses a number of features that may be advantageous to managers in human service settings. First, the approach delineates a variety of factors (DURABLE) that theory, research, and opinion as well as the author's experience suggest are important for managers to take into account when implementing programs. Recognition of these factors may provide managers with a broad-based view of implementation and a way of remembering important determinants of implementation. Second, specific program implementation procedures can be operationalized from the factors, and such procedures seem to help guide managers in the task of assuring that a program is implemented as planned. These kinds of features were ones reported by the majority of the human service program managers who participated in the potential user reaction procedure and given as reasons why they considered the approach to be potentially useful to them. A third feature of the approach, and an extremely important one, has to do with the fact that managers can be trained in the 14 program implementation procedures in a relatively short period of time (2-3 days). In support of this distinguishing feature, managers who have been trained in the approach have expressed satisfaction with their involvement in training and their experiences in applications following training.

The potential limitations of the approach may reflect issues of situational specificity. The investigations reported above occurred in public school organizations, with program managers who can be considered upper-level managers in those settings. Although program managers in other human service settings perceived the approach to have potential value, it is not currently known to what extent the approach might be effective in a broader array of human service organizations or useful for middle- and upper-level managers in business and industry.

The kind of approach to program implementation described above, though, may be considered important for the rapidly developing area of organizational behavior modification (OBM). Although research has demonstrated the OBM area as being a worthwhile addition to the larger domain of behavior modification and to organizational management fields, the majority of OBM interventions reported to date have been directed at line staff and paraprofessionals (Frederiksen & Lovett, 1980). There have been few reports of OBM approaches targeted to middle managers and executives, although the need for such studies, as a basis for charting new directions for OBM, has been seen as a priority research area (Frederiksen & Johnson, 1981; Frederiksen, 1982). Results of the two investigations reported above provide some initial and suggestive evidence of potentially effective ways of improving organizations by training managers who are in middle- and upper-level organizational positions in program implementation. The extent to which the particular approach described in the paper may be useful with a range of managers, including those in private business and industry, may be a useful empirical issue for OBM research.

Facilitating program implementation in organizations is a complex undertaking (Berman & McLaughlin, 1978; Glasser & Backer, 1980). Broad-based organizational intervention procedures seem necessary to facilitate implementation of programs in organizations. Hopefully, the approach described above will be informative to managers in human service and other kinds of organizations and spur additional investigations of this implementation technology.

REFERENCES

Berman, P., & McLaughlin, M. W. (1978). *Federal programs supporting educational change: Implementing and sustaining innovations*. Santa Monica, CA: Rand Corporation.

Bonoma, T. V. (1977). Overcoming resistance to changes recommended for operating programs. *Professional Psychology, 8*, 451-463.

Cronbach, L. J. (1982). *Designing evaluations of educational and social programs*. San Francisco: Jossey-Bass.

Davis, H. T., & Salasin, S. E. (1975). The utilization of evaluation. In E. L. Struening and M. Guttentag (Eds.), *Handbook of evaluation research*. Vol. 1, Beverly Hills, CA: Sage.

Frederiksen, L. W. Future directions for OBM. In L. W. Frederiksen (Ed.), *Handbook of organizational behavior management.* Wiley: New York, 1982.

Frederiksen, L. W., & Johnson, R. P. (1981). Organizational behavior management. In M. L. Hersen, R. Eisler, & P. Miller (Eds.), *Progress in behavior modification, 12,* 68-118. New York: Academic Press.

Frederiksen, L. W., & Lovett, S. B. (1980). Inside organizational behavior management: Perspectives on an emerging field. *Journal of Organizational Behavior Management, 2,* 193-203.

Fullan, M., & Pomfret, A. (1977). Research on curriculum and instruction implementation. *Review of Educational Research, 47,* 335-397.

Gibson, J. L., Ivancevich, J. M., & Donnelly, J. H. (1979). *Organizations: Behavior, structure, processes.* Dallas, TX: Business Publications, Inc.

Glasser, E. M., & Backer, T. E. (1980). Durability of innovations: How goal attainment scaling programs fare over time. *Community Mental Health Journal, 16,* 130-143.

Hauser, C. (1982). Evaluating replications. In J. D. Becklund (Ed.). *Strategies for change in special education: Maintaining and transferring effective innovations.* Program Development Assistance System: University of Washington.

Human Interaction Research Institute. (1976). *Putting knowledge to use: A distillation of the literature regarding knowledge transfer and change.* Los Angeles: HIRI.

Janis, I. I., & Mann, E. (1977). *Decision making.* New York: Free Press.

Joint Committee on Standards for Evaluation. (1981). *Standards for evaluations of educational programs, projects, and materials.* New York: McGraw-Hill.

Katz, D., & Kahn, R. L. (1979). *The social psychology of organizations.* 2nd Edition. New York: John Wiley & Sons.

Kratochwill, T. R., & Bergan, J. R. (1978). Evaluating programs in applied settings through behavioral consultation. *Journal of School Psychology, 16,* 375-386.

Leithwood, K. A., & Montgomery, D. J. (1980). Evaluating program implementation. *Evaluation Review, 4,* 193-214.

Maher, C. A. (1981). Improving the delivery of special education and related services in public schools. *Child Behavior Therapy, 3,* 29-44.

Maher, C. A., & Barbrack, C. R. (1980). A comprehensive framework for evaluation on the individualized education program. *Learning Disability Quarterly, 3,* 49-55.

Maher, C. A., & Barbrack, C. R. (1982). Preventing high school maladjustment: Comparison of professional and cross-age counseling approaches. *Behavior Therapy.*

Maher, C. A., & Barbrack, C. R. In press. Evaluating behavioral counseling using the goal attainment scaling approach. *Journal of School Psychology.*

Maher, C. A., & Bennett, R. E. In press. *Planning and evaluating special education services.* Englewood Cliffs, N.J.: Prentice-Hall.

Miller, L. M. (1978). *Behavior management: The new science of managing people at work.* New York: Wiley.

Patton, M. Q. (1978). *Utilization-focused evaluation.* Beverly Hills, CA: Sage.

Prue, D. M., & Frederiksen, L. W. (1982). Overcoming resistance to change. In L. W. Frederiksen (Ed.), *Handbook of Organizational Behavior Management.* New York: Wiley.

Wholey, J. S. (1980). *Evaluation: Promise and performance.* Washington, D.C.: Urban Institute.

A Case Study in the Programming and Maintenance of Institutional Change

Walter P. Christian

ABSTRACT. While behavior change projects and component analyses have been critical to the development of behavioral technology, behaviorists working in human service institutions have not focused enough attention on the "packaging" and systematic application of a technology for institutional change. In the present study, a package of organizational behavior management procedures was systematically introduced in a human service setting. The goal of intervention was to promote and maintain institutional change sufficient to support the wide scale implementation and maintenance of state-of-the-art behavioral procedures for program management and service delivery.

The specific procedures utilized in the study included the following: (1) planning; (2) establishing functional organizational structure; (3) recruiting, orienting, and training management and direct service personnel; (4) contracting for staff performance; (5) scheduling, supervising, and evaluating personnel; (6) obtaining and managing financial resources; (7) evaluating program operation; (8) ensuring legal safety; and (9) disseminating results.

Sixteen dependent variables, chosen to illustrate the quantity and quality of institutional change, were measured for the three years prior to, and five years following, intervention. Data from these measures indicated that intervention resulted in a positive change in virtually every aspect of program operation and that change resulting from the study was durable over time. Within the limitations imposed by case study design, these results were interpreted to suggest that institutional change is possible and that the technology required to effect such change is currently available.

The author wishes to acknowledge the support and cooperation provided by staff and Board of Trustees of the May Institute during the course of this investigation. The progress of institutional change at the May Institute is a direct result of the competence and dedication of these individuals. The author is also indebted to Stephen C. Luce, Peter J. Troy, Mary B. Norris, Marie E. Williams, and Priscilla A. Blew of the May Institute for their assistance in data analysis and in preparation of the manuscript. Reprints of this article can be obtained by writing Walter P. Christian, PhD, the May Institute, PO Box 703, Chatham, MA 02633.

99

INTRODUCTION

Human service programming has received a great deal of attention by behavioral researchers and practitioners. In particular, substantial progress has been made in the areas of program development, staff training and supervision, and behavioral assessment and evaluation (Kazdin, 1980). However, a wide discrepancy would appear to exist between the programs and procedures described in the literature and those routinely available to the consumer (Balthazar, 1972; Kazdin, 1979; Quilitch, 1975). It is becoming increasingly apparent that our ability to develop treatment programs and procedures has surpassed our ability to develop a human service system within which these programs and procedures can be effectively implemented and maintained (Krapfl, 1980; Quilitch, 1975; Reppucci, 1977).

The main reasons for this discrepancy would seem to be (1) a naïveté on the part of behavioral practitioners concerning the special constraints and obstacles characteristic of the human service institution (Hersen & Bellack, 1978a; Krapfl, 1980; Reppucci, 1977; Reppucci & Saunders, 1974); (2) a lack of skills on the part of the individual practitioner necessary to promote change and maintenance of change in the human service system (Christian & Hannah, 1983; Hersen & Bellack, 1978b; Krapfl, 1980); and (3) the absence of support from administration and/or staff for the wide scale implementation and maintenance of behavioral programming (Andrasik & McNamara, 1977; Hersen & Bellack, 1978a; Thompson & Grabowski, 1972).

These problems are further complicated by the lack of dissemination by behavioral practitioners of their effective models and strategies for changing the environments within which they work and for promoting change in the human service system as a whole. Furthermore, the literature that is available is dominated by demonstration projects and component analyses that stop short of wide scale implementation (e.g., across an institution as opposed to across clients or groups of clients) and/or maintenance for a significant period of time (e.g., three to five years as opposed to six to twelve months). Therefore, while behavior change projects and component analyses have been critical to the development of behavioral technology, behaviorists working in human service institutions have not focused enough attention on the "packaging" and systematic application of a technology for institutional change (Christian, 1981a; Reppucci, 1977).

This article describes a case study in which a package of organizational behavior management procedures was systematically introduced in a human service setting. The goal of intervention was to promote and maintain institutional change sufficient to support the wide scale implementation and maintenance of state-of-the-art behavioral procedures for program management and service delivery. The study was based upon the assumption that the most effective approach to changing a human service system is to introduce administrative structure, policy, and procedure consistent with the goals and objectives for change.

BACKGROUND AND PROBLEM DEFINITION

The study was conducted at The May Institute—a private, nonprofit human service program for autistic, severely disturbed youth. The Institute began as the Parents' School for Atypical Children in 1955. The center was founded by Dr. Jacques M. May, a physician, researcher, and author, well known for his work in public health and with the World Health Organization. Dr. May's mission reportedly was to develop a center where autistic children could be understood and rehabilitated.

The Institute is located on three acres in a residential section of Chatham—a town ninety miles southeast of Boston, Massachusetts on Cape Cod. In 1978, the Institute had an average census of 38 clients (6 to 16 years of age) with a staff of 60 (full time equivalent). At that time, the physical plant included five buildings containing dormitory space, classrooms, recreation area, dining facilities, and offices. Every area of the physical plant was in need of extensive repair and renovation, to the extent that state regulatory agencies were threatening to withhold approval of the program until renovation could be completed. Unfortunately, the Institute's budget at that time (FY 1979) did not provide support for extensive renovation and there was no prospect of additional revenue from grants or other sources.

State-of-the-art service programming for the Institute's client population (autistic children and adolescents) calls for "special educational programs using behavioral methods and designed for specific individuals" (Ritvo & Freeman, 1977). However, the Institute's philosophy of treatment prior to FY 1979 was not consistent with this criterion. In addition, staffing was inadequate to support intensive behavioral treatment programming and staff lacked the training and expertise sufficient to provide effective, individualized services to the client population. As a result, the average length of stay for clients discharged from the Institute during FY 1976-78 was 7 years, over 20% of the clients received psychotropic medication for behavioral control, and the quality and quantity of staff-to-client interaction were inadequate.

This situation was further complicated by inadequate organizational structure and personnel management methods. Administrative staff lacked sufficient expertise in human service management as well as in service programming for the client population. The limited organizational structure in effect prior to FY 1979 was ineffective and characterized by overlapping lines of authority and inadequate communication. For example, there were no in-house standards or criteria for program operation; no formal procedures for supervision, performance evaluation, and performance appraisal; no program evaluation system; and no systematic planning concerning how the program might be improved. These deficits contributed to high turnover of a minimally qualified work force, a problem that was further exacerbated by the absence of effective administrative leadership and support.

Finally, prior to institutional change, the Institute was not sufficiently committed to legal safety (e.g., no Human Rights Committee, no procedures for informing clients or guardians of their rights regarding treatment), applied research, fund raising, and public relations. Specifically, there was no systematic, appropriate use of expert consultation and peer review; no university affiliation to provide interns and practicum students as well as opportunities for staff to earn academic credit; no program of applied research; minimal grant writing activity; no staff commitment to professional development activity (e.g., membership in professional organizations, involvement in applied research and dissemination activity); no strategy for promoting good public relations (e.g., community-awareness projects); and inadequate communication between the Institute and its Board of Trustees and state officials responsible for the funding and regulation of program operation.

As a result of these deficiencies, the Institute was in danger of losing the support of its Board of Trustees, had poor credibility in its state's human service system, and was unable to obtain the additional funding needed to improve its situation. Despite the dedication and best intentions of its management and staff, the Institute had come to exhibit many of the problems characteristic of ineffective, "custodial" institutions (Christian, in press[a]; Horner, 1980;

Risley & Favell, 1979; *Wyatt v. Stickney*, 1972) and was apparently incapable of working out its predicament.

INTERVENTION

Institutional change at the May Institute was initiated in August, 1978, by its Board of Trustees. The Board hired the author as the program's Executive Director and authorized him to make whatever changes necessary to ensure that the Institute was provided with state-of-the-art administrative policy and procedure and that it became capable of providing services with the greatest likelihood of rehabilitating clients so that they could return to their homes and families. (The steps involved in developing this degree of Board support are described later in this section.)

A chronological description of the critical events in the process of institutional change has been provided in Table 1. Detailed descriptions of the procedures (e.g., goals and objectives, guidelines and sample forms, evaluation strategies) utilized in this process have been provided by Christian and Hannah (1983). The rationale for in-

TABLE 1

Critical Events During the Five-Year
Course of Institutional Change
Fiscal Year 1979

A.   Obtained support of Board of Trustees for the institutional change.
1.   Identified program's missions, goals, and objectives (i.e., to provide an environment in which autistic children can be rehabilitated to the greatest possible extent).
2.   Educated the Board concerning the fact that the program's goals and objectives could be attained only with a significant modification of current administrative policy and procedure and treatment methodology (i.e., obtaining Board support for behavioral administration and service delivery).
3.   Developed a two-year plan for comprehensive reorganization of the program in the form of an agreement between the Board of Trustees and the Executive Director (October, 1978). This agreement included the following major goals with specific timelines:

TABLE 1 (continued)

    a. Employment of management and service personnel with adequate training and expertise in the behavioral treatment of the client population.

    b. Development of an intensive, effective program of treatment for the client population based on the principles of behavior modification.

    c. Development of program evaluation and personnel management strategies sufficient to promote accountability, quality control, and legal safety.

    d. Emphasis on early intervention, community-based services, and transitional programming (short-term, intensive vs custodial).

    e. Commitment to fund raising, public relations, physical plant renovation, and applied research.

B. Replaced key management personnel.

    1. PhD behavioral psychologist to direct clinical and educational services employed in November, 1978.

    2. MBA health care administrator to coordinate administrative aspects of the program employed in April, 1979.

C. Initiated behavioral training for all direct service personnel in December, 1978, and conducted training at regular intervals throughout the course of institutional change.

D. Initiated fund raising efforts.

    1. Prioritized goals.

        a. Renovation of physical plant.

        b. Increased quantity and quality of management, middle management, and direct service staffing.

        c. Development of support service programs (e.g., parent training, language development, vocational training).

        d. Development of community-based group home and classroom programs.

    2. Researched foundation funding (Christian, 1982b) and procedures for obtaining adjustment in the program's annual tuition rate.

    3. Developed foundation grant proposal to support renovation of program's physical plant.

E. Initiated program evaluation procedures.

TABLE 1 (continued)

1. Ongoing Placheck ratings (Doke & Risley, 1972) of staff-to-client interaction.
2. Compilation of baseline data (FY 1976-1978) to permit an evaluation of the progress of institutional change.
F. Initiated biannual progress reporting to Board of Trustees.
G. Initiated annual external audit of program's accounting practices.
H. Developed Professional Advisory Board (Christian, 1983a). Initiated on-site consultation and peer review visits by experienced Ph.D. behavioral psychologists.
I. Established formal affiliation with the Department of Human Development, University of Kansas.

FISCAL YEAR 1980

A. Secured 62% adjustment (increase) in the program's tuition rate for the upgrading of the program's staff and services.
 1. Additional direct service and support service personne (20 FTE). Staff-to-client ratios increased from 2:7 to 2:: in classroom, from 1:4 to 1:3 in residential, and fror.. 1:8 to 1:5 in residential from 11:00 p.m. to 7:00 a.m.
 2. Competitive salary ranges and benefits for all existing and additional direct service personnel.
   a. Salaries increased from a flat rate of $7,000 to a salary range from $8,000 to $12,000.
   b. Benefits increased by more than 50%.
 3. Funding for partial renovation of the program's physical plant.
B. Recruited, oriented and trained additional personnel provided by rate adjustment.
C. Established policy, procedure, and supervision sufficient to ensure that (1) all new employees were oriented and trained in a timely, effective manner; and (2) existing staff received ongoing in-service training to ensure that their skills were maintained and further refined.
D. Obtained foundation grant to support the total renovation of the program's physical plant.
E. Initiated renovation of physical plant. (Renovation completed in FY 1982.)

TABLE 1 (continued)

F. Introduced comprehensive policy and procedure manual and revised organizational structure. (Format for policy and procedure manual and procedures for establishing organizational structure described by Christian and Hannah [1983].)

G. Introduced work performance contracting and forms and procedures for biannual performance evaluation and appraisal (written) for all staff.
  1. Initiated case manager system.
  2. Initiated weekly meetings of direct service, support service and administrative staff to review behavior change data and coordinate each client's treatment.
  3. Initiated regularly scheduled, formal orientation and training for staff.

H. Initiated development of a community-based group home.

I. Introduced procedures to ensure legal safety.
  1. Development of service agreements and authorization forms to ensure that each client (guardian) understands his or her rights and that those rights are protected in providing services.
  2. Initiation of client tracking and peer review systems to ensure that client progress is monitored and treatment plans are revised as necessary.

J. Initiated outreach parent training services (Czyzewski, Christian, and Norris, in press) with funding provided by foundation grants. (Permanent, ongoing funding for this project was obtained in FY 1981.)

K. Completed two-year plan initiated in October, 1978.

L. Developed new, more comprehensive work performance agreement between the Executive Director and the Board of Trustees (see description of this performance agreement).

M. Established formal affiliations with the Department of Psychology, West Virginia University.

FISCAL YEAR 1981

A. Established formal affiliations with Children's Hospital Medical Center, Boston, Massachusetts; Department of Psychology, University of Massachusetts; Department of Speech Pathology, Northeastern University.

TABLE 1 (continued)

B. Initiated vocational training and simulated workshop program with funding provided by foundation grants. (Permanent, ongoing funding for these services was obtained in FY 1982.)
C. Obtained funding (grant from state agency) for the construction of a community-based group home in cooperation with the local housing authority.
D. Introduced middle management personnel in direct services.
  1. Upgraded a senior employee in each residential unit to the position of Behavior Programming Specialist with supervisory authority over other employees in his or her residential unit.
  2. Upgraded a senior employee in each classroom to the position of Senior Teacher with supervisory authority over other teachers in his or her classroom.

FISCAL YEAR 1982

A. Added key administrative staff.
  1. PhD behavioral psychologist to supervise educational services (September, 1981).
  2. PhD behavioral psychologist to supervise transitional programming (social services, parent training, follow-up) (November, 1981.)
B. Introduced revised organizational structure with addition of new management personnel (see Figure 2).
C. Developed formal affiliations with the Department of Special Education, University of Vermont; the Graduate School, Lesley College, Cambridge, Massachusetts; and the Behavior Analysis and Therapy Program, Southern Illinois University, Carbondale, Illinois.
  1. Initiated internship for undergraduate special education students from the University of Vermont bringing six interns to the program each year for a full semester of practicum training.
  2. Initiated program with Lesley College to enable staff to take courses offered by the program's PhD psychologists for credit toward graduate degrees.

TABLE 1 (continued)

D. Obtained a grant for the purchase of computer, word processor, and graphics printing equipment. Initiated consultation to develop standardized, computerized curriculum for educational programming.

E. Initiated staff exchange program (involving three employees) with Green Line Teaching Homes, Inc. in Camarillo, California (Glahn & Christian, 1982).

F. Initiated community-based training programs designed to teach clients (1) appropriate shopping skills and (2) age-appropriate play skills (i.e., children were involved in a play group each week with "normal" children from the local community).

G. Developed and implemented a comprehensive program of transitional services that facilitated the discharge of clients to less restrictive settings and ensured the maintenance of their adjustment following discharge (Anderson, McGrale, Norris, Luce, & Christian, 1982; Luce, Anderson, Thibadeau, & Lipsker, in press).

H. Initiated consumer evaluation of program staff and services by parents of clients served by the program and social service/funding agencies concerned with clients' placement.

I. Developed and implemented policy and procedure for Human Rights Committee review of the program's facilities, staffing, and service programming.

J. Established Parent Advisory Board which held monthly meetings, published a quarterly newsletter, and advised the program's administrative staff on all aspects of service delivery.

K. Increased efforts to promote applied research and dissemination (Luce, Blew, & Thibadeau, 1983).
   1. Introduced an incentive system to provide bonus reinforcement (additional leave, cash, conference attendance) contingent upon staff involvement in research projects (Rotholz, Newsom, Luce, & Christian, 1982).
   2. Formalized planning and coordination of applied research through meetings, policy and procedure statements, and training sessions.
   3. Focused increased attention on the packaging and dissemination of results (e.g., via conference presenta-

TABLE 1 (continued)

tions, publications, etc.) (Blew, Luce, & Christian, 1982).

FISCAL YEAR 1983

A. Obtained funding to cover annual operating costs of group home through an adjustment in the program's tuition rate approved by its funding agencies.

B. Recruited and trained group home staff (teaching parents and assistants).

C. Completed construction of the group home; group home occupied by January, 1983.

D. Employed PhD behavioral psychologist to coordinate evaluation, research, and training activities.

E. Obtained foundation funding for a three-year early intervention project to begin in September, 1983 in association with Children's Hospital Medical Center, Boston, Massachusetts.

F. Moved six of the program's seven classrooms to leased space in a vacated public school facility which also housed Head Start services for neighboring communities.

G. Developed an Intensive Teaching Project designed to provide on-grounds, intensive instruction and one-to-one supervision for severely aggressive and self-injurious children incapable of being educated in a public school environment.

H. Initiated efforts designed to improve existing service programming as suggested by program evaluation data and consultant feedback.

1. Developed a staff training program featuring analysis of key tasks, competency-based training, and monitoring on-the-job performance of newly trained skills (Thibadeau, Butler, Gruber, Luce, Newsom, Anderson, & Christian, 1982).

2. Developed improved strategy for determining a client's treatment priorities and planning his or her course of treatment (Anderson, Luce, Newsom, Gruber, & Butler, 1983).

I. Increased efforts to package and disseminate programming and management technology (e.g., Christian, & Hannah, 1983; Christian et al., in press).

stitutional change was consistent with the literature concerning the implementation of behavioral programming strategies in human service institutions (e.g., Hersen & Bellack, 1978a; Reppucci, 1977; Tharp & Wetzel, 1969; and Thompson & Grabowski, 1972).

As previously described, the primary goal of the intervention was the establishment of administrative structure, policy, and procedure supportive of wide scale implementation and maintenance of behavioral treatment strategies. Procedures implemented during the course of institutional change included the following: (1) planning; (2) establishing an effective organizational structure; (3) contracting for an acceptable quantity and quality of staff performance; (4) recruiting, orienting, and training management, support service, and direct service personnel; (5) scheduling, supervising, and evaluating staff performance; (6) obtaining and managing financial resources; (7) evaluating program operation; (8) ensuring legal safety; (9) obtaining expert consultation and peer review; and (10) disseminating results.

Planning

As noted in Table 1, a two-year plan of goals and objectives for program reorganization was developed by the President of the Board of Trustees in consultation with the Executive Director in October, 1978. This became the Executive Director's temporary work performance contract. When the goals of the agreement were met to the satisfaction of the Board in September, 1979, the Executive Director developed a comprehensive list of performance standards for his position which was approved by the Board of Trustees. The criteria, procedures, timelines, and products specified in this document became the overall plan for the continued reorganization of the program.

In general, planning for institutional change included the activities of analysis, implementation, and measurement. *Analysis* included the operations of (1) defining, reviewing, and/or revising the program's mission; (2) assessing needs and resources; (3) specifying goals and objectives for change; and (4) identifying contingencies in operation in the program environment (i.e., positive and negative consequences responsible for shaping and maintaining desirable and undesirable aspects of program operation). *Implementation* involved (1) selecting procedural strategies; (2) preparing the environment for change (e.g., obtaining needed resources such as increased funding and qualified personnel), and (3) implementing procedures (i.e., determining baseline level of performance, determining how the procedure will be evaluated, applying the procedure, and programming maintenance and generalization). *Measurement* included the operations of (1) evaluating effectiveness (i.e., observing and recording, graphing and analyzing results); (2) communicating results; and (3) incorporating results.

One component of "preparing the environment for change," obtaining the support of the program's Board of Trustees, requires further explanation. The following procedures were followed in establishing such support: (a) literature was provided indicating the importance of institutional change and the effectiveness of the approach that was being proposed; (b) the support of consultants with recognized expertise in residential treatment programming, human service management, and institutional change was obtained (e.g., development of a professional advisory board as described by Christian, 1983a); (c) reference was made to recommendations of advocate groups and/or regulatory agencies concerning the need for institutional change and the potential effectiveness of the proposed model for promoting change; (d) performance agreements between the Executive Director and the Board of Trustees "required" that the program "be structured consistent with current legislation and ethical guidelines," and that it "utilize treatment procedures with a documented history of effectiveness with the client population" (i.e., behavioral treatment being the only approach that met this requirement for autistic clients); and (e) regular contact was maintained with Board members (meetings, regular written reports as described by Christian, 1981c) concerning all aspects of program operation, taking care to document the effectiveness of management procedures employed in promoting institutional change.

Establishing Organizational Structure

The organizational structure established during the course of the study was characterized by (1) centralization of authority; (2) formal rules and regulations for program operation; (3) specific work performance standards for program staff; (4) functional departmentalization; (5) small span of control (i.e., each supervisor responsible for a small number of subordinate personnel); and (6) flexibility for program staff to work in teams on special projects. Charts indicating the organizational structure of the program prior to intervention (June, 1978) and following intervention (June, 1983) are presented in Figures 1 and 2.

The choice of a formal, centralized organizational structure was based on the belief that such structure is necessary to ensure quality assurance and legal safety in human service settings. Human service settings, such as the one in the present study, are frequently characterized by a high-risk client population (i.e., severe handicapping condition, inability to advocate for their rights as clients) and a minimally qualified or inexperienced work force. Task specificity, functional departmentalization, and clear lines of authority were believed to be essential for safe, effective service delivery in such situations.

While a less formal, collegial organizational design may have provided greater flexibility for the program, it was feared that it might also result in a greater margin for error with regard to staff understanding and mastery of the tasks they were to perform and the control and supervision required to ensure that staff performance was efficient and effective. In addition, with the program already suffering from a lack of leadership and direction, it was felt that centralized control must be introduced. Furthermore, despite warnings by Wedel (1976) and others that formal, hierarchical structure "impedes effective responses to change," it was felt that the organizational structure implemented in the present study served to facilitate, rather than impede, the progress of institutional change.

It is important to note, however, that the effectiveness of centralized organizational structure in this case may have been due to the fact that the concept of project orientation was introduced to the organization via work performance standards. In this way, staff from several departments could work together on a special project (e.g., grant writing, applied research, publication and conference presentation activity) without the need for a horizontal organization being formally imposed as in the "matrix design" described by Wedel (1976) and Gray (1974). This "adaptive organizational structure" (Christian & Hannah, 1983) enabled the program to be flexible and problem-oriented without sacrificing functional specialization and centralized control.[1]

This type of structure was implemented through the development and utilization of (1) organizational charts; (2) policy and procedure manuals; (3) work performance contracting; (4) staff orientation and training; (5) committees and project teams; (6) staff meetings; (7) written communications; (8) consultation and peer review; and (9) performance evaluation and feedback. Evaluation of organiza-

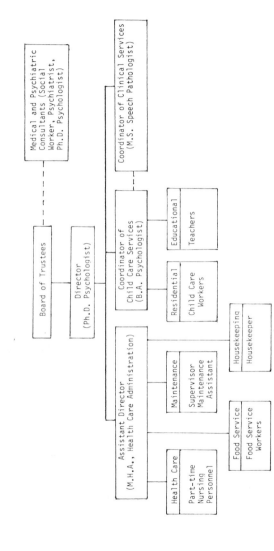

FIGURE 1. Chart of organizational structure in effect prior to the implementation of institutional change strategies (FY 1978).

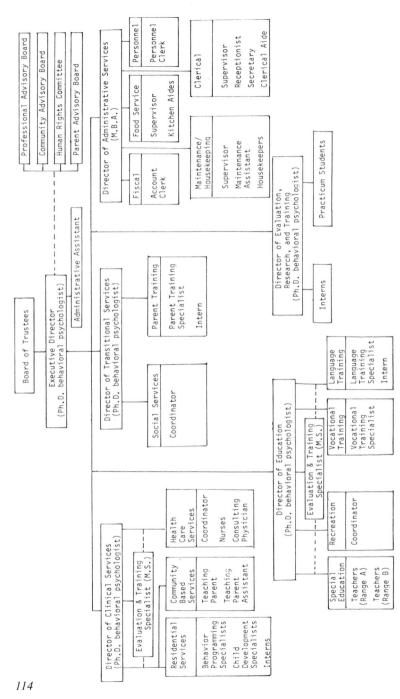

FIGURE 2. Chart of organizational structure in effect following the implementation of institutional change strategies (FY 1983).

tional structure was conducted to ensure that it was responsive to program need and effective in helping the program to meet its mission as well as the goals and objectives for institutional change. This was accomplished via written and verbal feedback from Board members, program staff, consultants, and consumers; testing, observation, and performance evaluation of program staff; evaluation of interdepartmental communications; and analysis of project team results as well as staff feedback concerning team function.

Work Performance Contracting

Work performance contracting involved the following procedures: (1) all goals and objectives of the program were translated into work assignments for management personnel who delegated assignments to other program staff via performance standards; (2) work assignments were clearly specified and called for some product or output from the employee within explicit time lines, thereby facilitating measurement and evaluation; (3) the number of personnel positions and the number of work assignments per position were minimized to the extent possible without jeopardizing the number of personnel and task specificity necessary to ensure that program goals and objectives were met; (4) performance standards called for performance consistent with (a) legal and ethical guidelines for human services, (b) the needs and best interests of the program's clients, and (c) the program's mission, goals, objectives, and available resources; and (5) performance standards were used to integrate the various components (departments) of the program's organizational structure as well as to reinforce its lines of authority and operational policies and procedures.

The most detailed work performance agreement was that between the Executive Director and the program's Board of Trustees. It specified goals, objectives, target behaviors, and timelines for every area of program operation; called for performance consistent with legal and ethical guidelines as well as with the available research literature pertinent to human service programming; and described the specific mechanisms that would be employed by the program in ensuring that legal and ethical criteria for service delivery were met.

The agreement was developed in FY 1980 and was used as the overall framework for completing the process of institutional change. It included descriptions of 70 tasks or performance objectives in 13 major categories:

    I. Administrative organization and personnel management
   II. Service programming
  III. Budget/accounting operations
  IV. Legal safety
   V. Program evaluation
  VI. Parent involvement
 VII. Maintenance and security of buildings, grounds, equipment, and supplies
VIII. Public relations
  IX. Fund raising
   X. Applied research
  XI. Utilization of consultants
 XII. University affiliations
XIII. Communication with Board of Trustees

The following are sample sections from this document chosen to illustrate the key tasks in institutional change: administrative organization and personnel management, behavioral service programming, program evaluation, and applied research.

I. *Administrative organization and personnel management.* Management of administrative structure and staff sufficient to support a progressive, comprehensive program of human services for the client population. Direction of administrative, direct service, clinical support and support service staff with education, training, and certification (if applicable) sufficient to meet or exceed the requirements of pertinent state and federal licensing and funding agencies concerning personnel and the quality and quantity of services provided.

    A. Recruitment, orientation, direct supervision and evaluation of administrative staff (for example, (directors of clinical services; education; administrative support services; transitional services; and evaluation, research, and training). Assist administrative staff in recruitment, orientation, supervision and evaluation of direct service staff (teachers and residential staff) and support service staff (clerical, food service, and maintenance personnel).
       1. Orientation of new personnel completed within first week of their employment.

2. Training of new personnel completed within first month of their employment.
3. Written work performance standards for each employee appropriate to the needs of the program, the skills of the employee, and pertinent regulatory and licensing requirements of supervisory agencies signed by the employee, his or her direct supervisor, and the Executive Director within the first six weeks of an individual's employment. Employee's work performance standards reviewed or revised when necessary and at the anniversary date of an individual's employment; written agreement of employee, direct supervisor, and Executive Director required for revision of standards.
4. Written evaluation of each employee's performance relative to the standards specified for his or her position, completed and approved in writing by the employee, his or her supervisor, and the Executive Director at six-month intervals from date of employment.
5. Weekly individual meeting conducted with each member of administrative staff and bimonthly meetings with the general staff to provide clinical consultation, ongoing communication, in-service training, and/or clarification of program policy and procedures.
6. Staff performance monitored daily in visits to residential, classroom, and other areas of the physical plant.

B. Comprehensive manual of personnel policy and procedures describing all aspects of program operation submitted to the Board of Trustees for review on an annual basis.
C. Current and complete personnel files for each employee maintained as per regulatory agency requirements and in-house standards.
D. Salary range for each position specified as per regulatory agency requirements; competitive salaries and benefits provided for all staff within the limits of the program budget.
E. Current profile of the program staff included in the bi-annual report to the Board of Trustees. Profile to include: (1) positions; (2) name(s) of employee(s) at each position; (3) salary range for each position; and (4) employee's highest academic degree and certification (if applicable).

F. Adherence to Equal Opportunity/Affirmative Action and regulatory agency guidelines concerning all aspects of personnel management.

II. *Service programming.* Comprehensive, least restrictive human services geared to the special needs of clients in the program provided consistent with (a) the needs of the individual client; (b) current research literature on the education and treatment of the client population; (c) recommendations from the program's Professional Advisory Board (see section XI); (d) supervisory agency regulations concerning quality and quantity of clinical, educational, transitional, and administrative services; (e) requests from parents and referral agencies; (f) the client's approved individual educational plan; and (g) accepted legal/ethical guidelines concerning the provision of human services.

A. Initial assessment of each new admission completed within first six weeks; assessment to include appropriate standardized instruments as well as observation of each client in home (when possible), residential, classroom, and community settings. Follow-up assessments using the same instruments and procedures made at six-month intervals and/or when service is terminated.

B. Treatment plan for each client completed within first month of admission specifying (a) target behaviors (based on behavioral and/or medical assessment) in areas of health maintenance and communication, social, motor, academic, and self-care skills; (b) treatment procedures to be employed; (c) alternative procedures attempted (in the case of a restrictive procedures to be employed); (d) goals and objectives for treatment; (e) criteria for success; (f) method of evaluating progress; (g) reasonable risks and benefits of the procedure; and (h) authorization from parent/legal guardian.

C. Treatment procedures of demonstrated effectiveness used as per the specifications of the client's treatment plan; utilization of the least restrictive procedure.

D. Each client's progress reviewed at three-month intervals, with review addressing target behaviors on treatment plan and progress toward objectives specified. Written report of each client's progress provided parents/legal guardians and/or referral agencies at three-month intervals from date of admission.

E. Treatment plan revised as indicated by review of progress to ensure that each client is receiving *effective* treatment based upon his/her needs.

F. Written summary of behavioral assessment and quarterly progress notes entered in each client's case record (see Section IV).

G. Existing service programs improved and new ones developed to ensure progressive service programming (e.g., community-based group homes, specialized foster parent programs, and community-based consultation/training services for parents and helping professionals).

V. *Program evaluation.* Ongoing program evaluation, accountability, and quality control—utilizing accepted evaluation practices, reliability checks, and validation procedures—effective in monitoring the following: (a) Demographic and treatment status data for clients served (age, length of stay, etc.); (b) graphical presentation indicating the efficacy of services provided to each client (the efficacy of the specific procedure employed to treat a specific target behavior); (c) the restrictiveness of the procedures employed; (d) client status at follow-up; (e) the program's success in meeting its goals and objectives as specified by the Board of Trustees/state officials; (f) cost effectiveness and budgeting/accounting practices; (g) social validity and consumer satisfaction; (h) record-keeping procedures; (i) staff training and employee work performance; (j) program's impact on human services in general; (k) outcome of applied research projects; (l) protection of client rights; (m) outcome of grant projects as per requirements of funding agency; (n) success of fund raising and public relations efforts; (o) success of parent involvement and parent training efforts (if applicable); and (p) compliance with guidelines of state and federal regulatory agencies.

A. Procedural description and results of ongoing in-house evaluation and peer review on each of the areas listed above included in biannual reports to the Board of Trustees (see Section XIII).

B. Periodic outside evaluation conducted by recognized experts in the fields of health and human services; written reports submitted to the Board of Trustees summarizing findings and recommendations of each outside evaluator (see Section XI).

C. Ongoing revision of program's services, policy and procedures made as per the results of program evaluation efforts (for example, going to a new treatment procedure when evaluation indicates present procedure ineffective in meeting treatment plan objectives).

X. *Applied research.* Direction of applied research designed to (a) improve the effectiveness of program services; (b) determine more effective individual and group training procedures for use with the program's client population; (c) investigate new administrative and staff training/orientation systems effective in making human services more progressive; and (d) facilitate the return of the client to his/her family and home community.

A. A Human Rights Committee consisting of members of the local community and helping professionals developed for the purpose of considering the reasonable risks and benefits to clients who are to be involved as subjects in applied research conducted by program staff. A description of the current membership and the function of the committee submitted to the Board of Trustees as a part of each biannual report (see Section XIII).

B. The program's applied research to be conducted according to guidelines established by the American Psychological Association and those included in the following publications:

1. Protection of human subjects: Policies and procedures. *Federal Register*, November 16, 1973, *38*, No. 221.

2. Protection of human subjects: Research involving children. *Federal Register*, July 21, 1978, *43*, No. 141.

C. At least two major research projects completed each year, using experimental control rigorous enough to ensure the reliability and replicability of results. Reports on the progress of ongoing applied research included in biannual reports to the Board of Trustees.

D. At least two grant proposal(s) for the support of applied research submitted each year.

E. Preparation of summary reports of each research project for publication in professional journals and/or presentation at professional conferences.[2]

Work performance standards for the Executive Director provided an overall framework for specifying work assignments and performance standards for all program staff. For example, following the organizational structure presented in Figure 2, personnel management and budget/accounting tasks in the Executive Director's agreement served as the nucleus of the performance standards for the Director of Administrative Services. Similarly, service programming and personnel management tasks were used to develop performance standards for the Director of Clinical Services and the Director of Education; Sections VI (Case Records and Clients' Rights) and VI (Parent Involvement) were delegated via work performance standards for the Director of Transitional Services. Sample work performance standards for these key administrative positions have been provided elsewhere (Christian & Hannah, 1983).

Similarly, work performance standards for administrative staff were used to develop descriptions of tasks to be performed by direct service personnel. For example, performance agreements for residential and educational staff specified 25 tasks in ten major categories including:

I.   Treatment planning and service delivery
II. Health care
III. Communication with parents, legal guardians, and representatives of concerned social service and funding agencies.
IV. Maintenance of the environment
V.   Off-grounds activities
VI. Understanding and utilization of behavioral treatment procedures
VII. Communication with administrative and support service personnel
VIII. Legal safety for clients and their families
IX. Public relations
X.   Case manager system (if applicable)

Case manager system. A strategy that was particularly effective in increasing the quality and quantity of staff-to-client interaction as well as in ensuring a commitment to data collection/analysis and applied research was the *case manager system.* In this system, the more experienced members of the direct service staff were assigned (via performance contracting) the additional task of serving as "case managers" for the program's clients. The case manager, in consultation with other program staff, was responsible for (1) assessing a client's needs; (2) setting goals and objectives for treatment; (3) planning, conducting, and evaluating the success of *behavior change projects*; (4) documenting change in the client's case record (e.g., graphical representations, progress notes, etc.); (5) assisting in transitional planning for the client (e.g., discharge and follow-up); (6) communicating with parents/legal guardians; and (7) generally monitoring the client's program of services to ensure that his or her needs were being met and rights were being protected.

The *behavior change project* was the product or output of the case manager system. Each project involved the following tasks which were specified in work performance standards for direct service personnel serving as case managers:

1. *Baseline assessment* of the client's behavior to indicate his or her treatment needs as well as to serve as a basis for evaluating the change (or lack of change) in the client's behavior in response to treatment.
2. Determination of a *goal for treatment* with an explicit *criterion for success.*
3. Utilization of an *evaluation procedure* sufficient to enable program staff to reliably determine (a) if the treatment administered or service delivered actually had some effect on the client's behavior, and (b) if change seen in the client's behavior or baseline condition was reliably a result of the treatment administered or service delivered. Minimum of two reliability checks conducted for each phase—baseline, intervention, follow-up—of a behavior change project.
4. Implementation of a treatment procedure or delivery of a service using *procedures of demonstrated effectiveness* when used with individuals having a condition and presenting problem similar to the client's.
5. *Measurement, analysis, and documentation* of the results of treatment or service delivery with ongoing peer review pro-

vided by other members of the program staff (administrative *and* direct service) at weekly treatment team meetings (see page 81) and by professional consultants during their site visits.

6. *Maintenance and generalization* of treatment results by continuing to monitor the client's progress and by enlisting the support of other program staff.

7. *Completion of a behavior change project form* documenting the rationale, procedures, and results of each behavior change project.

A form was used to document the initiation, progress, and completion of behavior change projects. The following is an example of this form:

BEHAVIOR CHANGE PROJECT

Name of Client:_____

Start date:_____

End date:_____

Specific Behavior: Coin Value Recognition
Definition: When presented with a quarter and asked "How many cents?" the client will respond "25 cents."
Terminal Objective: Shopping
Skill Area: (1)Social (2)Language (3)Motor (4)Academic (5)Transitional (6)Self-Help (circle one)
Acquisition Criteria: 80% correct for 3 consecutive blocks of ten trials
Procedures:

1. Baseline: Present quarter and ask "How many cents?"—no feedback given—praise good sitting, etc.
2. Acquisition: Present quarter, ask "How many cents?" If correct, reinforce with praise and cereal. If incorrect, answer given, model, correct response and have child say "25 cents," then reinforce.
3. Generalization: Steps below to be carried out once daily.

Settings	Persons	Language Cues	Materials
1. Classroom	Staff A	"How many cents?"	New quarter
2. House	Staff B	"How much is this?"	Tarnished Quarter
3. Yard	Staff C	"What is this worth?"	Medium worn quarter

4. Maintenance: Post-check data taken every Monday and Friday.

Reinforcer: Praise and cereal during continuous reinforcement (crf); fade to praise on intermittent schedule.
Reinforcement Schedules: Crf; fade to once daily.
Potential risks of the program: Failure to acquire coin value; mild tantrums (crying) in response to prompts.
Additional agreements/person responsible: Classroom and house staff.
Approval obtained from parent/legal guardian.*

_____   _____
                                          May Institute Representative
*Parent/legal guardian approval of treatment plan (IEP) and goals authorize conduct of behavior change projects. Additional signature/approval required if treatment involves use of restrictive isolation, physical restraint, or any procedure potentially harmful to the child. (See Human Rights Committee Guidelines.)
Results: A. The objective was met/not met
          B. The staff was satisfied/dissatisfied with the results
          C. Criterion for generalization was met/not met
             (circle one)
Data: Attach graph of all data pertinent to this project. Include results of reliability checks conducted during each phase of the project.

*Supervisor Approval:*_____   _____
                          Name   Date
This kind of operational specificity and consistency contributed to program accountability and quality control. In addition, since program management (behavioral psychologists) was familiar with this operational framework, it was able to effectively train, supervise, and evaluate staff performance within a similar framework. In short, it was possible for employees in all areas of the program to

become more product-oriented in their jobs and to utilize a more systematic, problem-solving approach to their work assignments.

Staff Orientation and Training

As previously described, orienting employees to the tasks they were to perform was accomplished by developing performance standards for their jobs and by negotiating and contracting with each employee for an acceptable level of performance. Orienting an employee to the work environment was accomplished by the use of an *orientation checklist*, a procedure which routed each new employee to administrative staff who provided the employee with information about their specific areas of responsibility. Research indicated that the orientation checklist was (1) more effective in equipping the employee with information about the program, and (2) more preferred by both new employees and administrative staff than more traditional group orientation sessions (Christian & Troy, 1983).

Formal training for all new staff was conducted within the first four to six weeks of their employment, although the employee received intensive on-the-job training from more experienced staff from the start of his or her employment. Job analysis via written questionnaires and direct observation determined the skills that were taught. A training plan specified objectives, methods, and instructional procedures for each session and trainers (PhD and masters-level personnel) were required to rehearse their instructional procedures for peer review and feedback.

Training was typically conducted in an intensive three-day workshop format with new employees required to read selected articles prior to training and to complete a data-based behavior change project within four to six weeks of completing the workshops. Attendance at professional conferences and on-site presentations by visiting consultants were also used to supplement training workshops. For example, beginning in FY 1980, from 25 to 50 employees attended state, regional, and national conferences and conventions each year with financial support provided by the program.

The following is an example of the three-day staff training workshops conducted at three- to six-month intervals during the course of institutional change as well as when needed for the orientation and training of new personnel.

STAFF TRAINING SCHEDULE
DAY 1

Topic	Instructor
1. Overview of the program	Executive Director (PhD)
*2. Program policies and procedures	Director of Administrative Services (MBA)
*3. Case manager system	Evaluation and Training Specialist (MS)
*4. Medical information	Coordinator of Health Care Services (RN)
*5. Behavioral characteristics of autistic children	Director of Education (PhD)
6. Supervised practicum training in 1:1 interaction with autistic children	Director of Research, Evaluation and Training (PhD); Evaluation and Training Specialist

DAY 2

*1. Clients rights and legal safety	Executive Director	
2. Treatment team meetings	Evaluation and Training Specialist	
3. Office protocol	Administrative Assistant (MS)	
*4. Data collection methods	Director of Research, Evaluation & Training	
*5. Developing functional treatment objectives	"	
*6. Discrete trial training	"	
7. Group (1:3; 1:4) teaching methods	"	
*8. Measurement and reliability	"	
*9. Single subject research design	"	
10. Developing functional short-term objectives	"	
*11. Graphing and data analysis	"	

*12.	Language acquisition Sign language Incidental teaching	Language Training Specialist (BS)
13.	Supervised practicum training in 1:1 instruction with autistic children	Director of Research, Evaluation and Training; Evaluation and Training Specialist

DAY 3

*1.	Generalization and maintenance of behavior change	Director of Research Evaluation & Training
2.	Current research projects; program policy and procedure concerning applied research	"
*3.	Reliability and advanced research design	Director of Clinical Services (PhD)
*4.	Mild treatment procedures to reduce behavior (e.g., overcorrection, positive practice, contingent effort)	"
*5.	Negative reinforcement, escape motivation, sensory reinforcement and extinction	Director of Education
6.	Supervised practicum training in 1:1 instruction with autistic children	Director of Research, Evaluation, and Training; Evaluation and Training Specialist

*Involved reading assignments such as Christian (1981d), Hall (1975), Luce and Christian (1981).

The effectiveness of training was evaluated by monitoring trainee performance. This was accomplished using strategies such as behavioral observation, situational testing, written tests and quizzes, and assignments and special projects (e.g., the completion of a data-based behavior change project with a particular client). Care was also taken to assess trainee attendance, participation, and satisfaction. Maintenance and generalization of training effectiveness was promoted by contingent feedback for staff performance, going from continuous to intermittent performance feedback, cueing or prompting desired performance, and providing ongoing supervision and training throughout an individual's employment.

Supervision

Each individual was supervised by a senior, more experienced employee in his or her immediate work environment. For example, each residential unit or cottage was staffed with a supervising "Behavior Programming Specialist" (masters-level or experienced bachelors-level employee) and a number of "Child Development Specialists" (staff to client ratio of 3:8 in FY 1983 as opposed to a ratio of 1:4 in FY 1978). Each classroom was staffed with a supervising "Senior Teacher" and a number of "Teachers" (staff-to-client ratio of 2:5 in FY 1983 as opposed to 2:7 in FY 1978). Staffing ratios in each of these environments were periodically improved with the addition of interns and practicum students involved in onsite training.

The specific strategies utilized to supervise and evaluate program staff have been described in considerable detail elsewhere (Christian & Hannah, 1983). Briefly, these strategies included (1) recruiting a competent supervisory staff (behavioral PhD psychologists as department heads, experienced masters-level behaviorists as support service and senior direct service personnel); (2) orienting and training supervisory as well as support service staff; (3) developing a professional work force; (4) utilizing routines and checklists; (5) establishing and maintaining an effective feedback loop; (6) obtaining professional consultation and peer review; and (7) conducting regular performance appraisal and providing feedback to staff.

The development of a professional work force was particularly useful in promoting institutional change. This began with the selection of job titles that communicated management's expectation of each employee while providing task identity and prestige for the employee. For example, titles such as "child development specialist" replaced the more traditional titles of "child care worker" or "attendant."

Another step was to provide each employee with as much autonomy and opportunity for self-management as possible. As previously described, this was accomplished through work performance contracting: Individualized work performance standards for each employee; employee participation in goal selection; the case manager system in which each employee coordinated a client's treatment program; and work on special projects negotiated by the employee with his or her supervisor. Similarly, in regular meetings and feedback sessions, the employee was allowed input in decision-making that affected his or her job or immediate work environment.

Ongoing staff development was also considered essential to the establishment and maintenance of a professional work force. Therefore, the program initiated the practice of budgeting the equivalent of approximately 2% of its total personnel cost each year ($10,000 to $30,000) for the purposes of staff development. The majority of this funding was used to support the following types of staff development activities: (a) Staff attendance at professional workshops and conferences both in and out of state; (b) payment of cash bonuses or other special awards for above-standard job performance or for work related to career development (e.g., partial payment of tuition for graduate study completed during one's employment); (c) exposure of staff to external consultants with expertise relative to some aspect of their (staff's) work or career development; and (d) provision of resources to assist staff in their work performance (e.g., routines or checklists to facilitate task completion, supplies and materials, equipment such as computers and copying machines, audiovisual recorders, etc.). Other types of staff development activity included: (a) Development of a small library to assist staff in their work; (b) encouragement of staff involvement in research and program development; (c) ongoing orientation and in-service training to ensure that staff were exposed to the most current human service technology, career development opportunities, etc; (d) establishment of affiliations with universities and other human service programs so that academic credit and practicum experience could be arranged for qualified staff; and (e) job rotation so that each employee had maximum exposure to other tasks and individuals in the program environment and, hopefully, increased opportunities to develop new skills and varied career interests.

Communication. Weekly interdisciplinary/interdepartmental treatment team meetings facilitated communication and helped to ensure consistency of treatment efforts. These meetings were scheduled and conducted as follows:

TREATMENT TEAM MEETING

Attendees

Service staff (direct and support service personnel from class-rooms and residential units) working with a particular group of clients; supervisors of service departments represented; other staff (e.g., administrative personnel, consultants, staff from other treatment teams) by invitation.

Scheduling. Weekly; written schedule posted monthly.
Duration. One hour, unless special arrangements made.
Supervision. Meeting run by supervisors of departments represented.
Agenda. Prearranged case presentations; brief review of each client's treatment and progress (e.g., analysis of graphs); revisions of treatment plan (if needed); feedback from staff; feedback from department supervisor; announcement of next scheduled meeting; assignment of case presentations.
Products. Attendance register; record of treatment plan and behavior change project changes; participation ratings.
Additional features. Manual including each client's current treatment plan, behavior change projects, and graphs of pertinent data available to facilitate discussion; refreshments; relaxed atmosphere; peer and supervisory feedback contingent upon staff attendance and participation.[3]

Performance Evaluation and Appraisal

The following sources of data were used to evaluate staff performance:

A. Staff Behavior
　1. Activity
　　*a. Employee attendance records
　　*b. Daily monitoring and recording of employee performance (e.g., using "pla-check" method developed by Doke & Risley, 1972).
　　c. Shift change checklist (a form completed by staff at the end of their shift to promote communication and consistency with the incoming shift).
　　*d. Minutes of treatment team meetings.

2. Productivity
   *a. Client progress reports
   *b. Behavior change project forms
   c. Daily monitoring and recording
   *d. Written correspondence to, and records of interviews with, supervisor
   *e. Minutes and participation ratings from treatment team meetings
3. Satisfaction
   *a. Staff satisfaction ratings
   b. Records of staff turnover and absenteeism

B. Client Progress
1. Activity
   a. Behavior change project forms
   b. Client status reports (summary of each client's service plan reviewed and updated at treatment team meetings and circulated to staff on a weekly basis)
   c. Daily monitoring and recording of client behavior (e.g., pla-check ratings)
   d. Shift change checklists
   e. Minutes of treatment team meetings
   f. Client's case record
2. Progress
   a. Graphed data from extended periods of daily monitoring and recording
   b. Behavioral assessment results (e.g., periodic assessment using instruments such as the *Adaptive Behavior Scale*, Nihira, Foster, Shellhaas, & Leland [1974]).
   c. Quarterly progress reports
   d. Behavior change project forms
   e. Minutes of treatment team meetings
   f. Client's case record
3. Satisfaction
   a. Satisfaction ratings and feedback from parents and concerned persons
   b. Satisfaction ratings from referral and funding agencies[4]

Data available from these sources made it possible for supervisors (department heads) to provide staff with reliable, highly specific feedback in individual meetings and biannual written performance evaluations. Staff also received frequent verbal and written feedback from the supervisor in their immediate work environment (Senior Teachers and Behavior Programming Specialists). Sources of data marked with an asterisk (*) were considered most important in evaluating staff performance. Permanent product data from each of these areas were used by supervisors in rating employee performance.

Supervisors were trained and monitored by the Executive Director to ensure that they were capable of providing feedback to staff in a positive, educational manner. Feedback addressed interpersonal skills and diplomacy, performance criteria and job results, and recommendations concerning future performance. Staff were given an opportunity to respond to feedback as well as to provide feedback to their supervisor concerning his or her performance. Follow-up evaluation and feedback was also provided.

In addition to annual salary increases (merit and cost of living) which were based on satisfactory performance evaluations, staff received bonus rewards (e.g., cash, additional leave, partial payment of graduate school tuition) contingent upon outstanding work performance and involvement in applied research as documented in point systems and by the direct observations of their supervisors. Staff were also rewarded with opportunities for job rotation (e.g., a teacher's being given the opportunity to do 1:1 language training one day each week) and career development (e.g., trips to professional conferences, funding for research projects, involvement in staff exchange activity with other programs, involvement in continuing education workshops).

Fund Raising

Two types of fund raising strategies were employed: rate adjustment and foundation grants. Rate adjustment involved the program's seeking to increase its operating budget by obtaining an increase in the annual tuition rate it charged for its services. Each year the program was required to submit a comprehensive cost report to the state's Rate Setting Commission. After the total "allowable" costs for the reporting year were determined and an adjustment was made for inflation, the adjusted cost figure was divided by the program's average monthly client census for the reporting year. This calculation yielded an "approved annual tuition rate" which the program could charge for serving each client. This rate was paid by local school districts and social service agencies, individually or in a cooperative, "split funding" arrangement.

For a program to increase its rate above the figure yielded by this calculation, it must obtain the approval of its "major purchaser" (the agency responsible for funding the greatest number of clients); in this case, either the state Department of Education or the Department of Social Services. Therefore, the program was required to make a formal proposal to one of these agencies justifying its request for increased funding. This strategy was employed on three occasions during the course of institutional change resulting in a 62.1% rate increase in FY 1980, 5.5% in FY 1982, and 4.2% in FY 1983.

The second fund raising strategy, obtaining foundation grants, was made possible by the program's being able to qualify as a tax-exempt, private, non-profit corporation as per the regulations of the Internal Revenue Service. All grants were written by the Executive Director in association with other members of the program staff. The specific procedures which were followed in grant preparation and submission have been described by Christian (1982b).

It is important to note that at no time during the period of institutional change was the program dependent upon foundation grants. As a rule, foundation grants were used to demonstrate the effectiveness of a new service program or project so that a rate adjustment could be justified to provide ongoing, "hard" funding for program development. This enabled the program to obtain ongoing funding for an upgrading of the quality and quantity of its personnel, renovation of its physical plant, transitional services (including parent training and in-home consultation), vocational training, operating costs for its community-based group home, and location of classrooms in a public school facility. In this way, if grant funding was interrupted or discontinued for any reason, the basic operation of the program was not affected.

Legal Safety

An important component of institutional change involved the development and implementation of strategies to ensure that the program's clients were served in accordance with their legal rights. First, criteria for legally safe human service programming were identified by reviewing the available literature (e.g., Hannah,

Christian, & Clark, 1981; Martin, 1981; Sheldon-Wildgen & Risley, 1982), ethical codes of professional organizations (e.g., American Psychological Association, 1977; Association for the Advancement of Behavior Therapy, 1978), and guidelines promulgated by regulatory agencies (e.g., Joint Commission for the Accreditation of Hospitals, 1978) and client advocacy groups (e.g., American Civil Liberties Union).

Second, the status of the program was determined relative to those criteria. The areas found to be in greatest need of attention concerned the establishment of formal policies and procedures governing service delivery and clients' rights protection, and the utilization of external consultation and peer review.

Finally, specific strategies were implemented in an effort to enable the program to operate consistent with legal safety criteria. These included procedures designed to (1) educate the client (guardian) about his or her rights and the responsibility of the program to protect them; (2) ensure that the clients' rights to informed consent and confidentiality were protected; (3) provide regular reviews of treatment plans and procedures by a Human Rights Committee; and (4) train and monitor staff performance to ensure that clients' rights were protected (cf. Christian, in press [b]). In each of these areas, forms, audiovisual aides, and procedural guidelines were developed and systematically implemented.

OUTCOME MEASUREMENT

Sixteen dependent variables were measured for the three years prior to, and the five years following, intervention. Outcome data were obtained from rating forms and written records which were carefully checked to ensure their reliability. Dependent measures, sources, measurement methods, and reliability scores for the data reported in the study are presented in Table 2. In general, several sources of information (e.g., client case records, biannual reports, audited financial records) were examined by independent raters in recording data for each dependent measure (e.g., average length of stay for clients discharged) for each fiscal year from 1976 through 1983. For each measure, the number of rater agreements was divided by the total number of rater agreements and disagreements and multiplied by 100%.

As indicated in Table 2, interrater reliability scores ranged from

Table 2

Dependent Measures, Measurement Methods, and

Reliability Scores for Data Reported in the Study

Dependent Measure	Source of Data	Method of Measurement	Interrater Reliability Total Number of Ratings	Score
Operating Budget (excluding grants) (Figure 3)	Audited financial records; Rate Setting Commission documents; biannual board reports	Listing of operating budget by year from one source, checked against other sources by independent raters.	8 (budget per year)	100%
Funding from grants (Figure 3)	Same as above	Listing of grant amount received each year from one source and checked against other sources by independent raters.	22 (grants) 8 (total amount per year)	100% 100%
Cost effectiveness (figure 4)	Same as above	(Annual operating budget ÷ annual operating census) X average length of stay for clients served calculated for each year and adjusted for inflation by independent raters.	8 (program cost quotient per year)	100%
Total number of employees (FTE) (Figure 5)	Same as above	Listing of annual FTE by independent raters	8 (average FTE per year)	100%
Employee salary (Figure 5)	Same as above	Total salaries for each year divided by the average number of staff (FTE) for the year; calculation of % increase for each year relative to FY 1976 by independent raters.	8 (average salary per year) 8 (average % increase in salary per year relative to FY 1976)	100% 100%
Staff Turnover (Figure 5)	Personnel files; forms completed at the time of resignation; biannual board reports	Listing of the names of employees leaving employment by year summed and divided by the total staffing (FTE) for that year X 100%. Calculations by independent raters.	8 (rate of turnover per year)	88%
Presentations and publications (Figure 6)	Copies of articles, books, professional journals; conference brochures; bibliographies (e.g., Blew, Williams & Christian, 1982); biannual board reports	Separate frequency counts for presentations and publications each year from one source checked against other sources by independent raters.	8 (total number of presentations per year) 8 (total number of publications per year)	88% 100%
Number of clients receiving psychotropic medication (Figure 7)	Physicians' orders; medication logs; medical records; clients' case records	Names of clients on medication as of July 1 each year from one source and checked against other sources by independent raters.	35 (number of clients) 8 (total per year)	100% 100%

Table 2 (Continued)

Dependent Measure	Source of Data	Method of Measurement	Interrater Reliability Total Number of Ratings	Score
Total number of clients discharged (Figure 8)	Clients' case records; biannual board reports; monthly census reports	Same as above	47 (names of clients) 8 (total per year)	100% 100%
Number of clients discharged to home or foster home (Figure 8)	Clients' case records; responses to parent question-naires; telephone check; biannual board reports.	Clients' names and placement after discharge listed by year and checked against parent questionnaires and telephone contacts by independent raters.	24 (names of clients)	100%
Length of stay for clients discharged (Figure 8)	Clients' case records; biannual board reports; monthly census reports.	Difference between admission date and discharge date calculated (years & months) and listed for each client discharged by year; mean calculated for each year by independent raters.	160 (admission and discharge dates for random sample of 10 clients each year) 8 (average per year)	98% 100%
Length of stay for clients served (Figure 8)	Clients' case records; treatment contracts; biannual board reports	Calculation of time elapsed between client's admission and June 1 of each year; mean calculated for each year by independent raters	80 (admission dates for random sample of 10 clients each year) 8 (average per year)	98% 88%
Client census (average census) (Table 3)	Audited financial records; Rate Setting Commission documents; biannual board reports	Listing of average monthly census per year by independent raters.	8 (average monthly census per year)	100%
Staff-to-client interaction (Table 3)	Direct observation	Placheck rating on a variable time basis by independent raters across several days. Agreements as to # of children involved in interaction divided by total # of children present (Doke & Risley, 1972).	48 (number of classroom/ residential unit obser-vations)	95%
Recidivism (number of clients dis-charged to home/ foster home requiring further residential treatment) (Table 3)	Responses to parent question-naires; telephone check	Clients' names and current placement listed by year by independent raters.	24 (names of clients) 8 (total per year)	100% 100%

Table 2 (Continued)

Dependent Measure	Source of Data	Method of Measurement	Interrater Reliability	
			Total Number of Ratings	Score
Consumer satisfaction (Table 3)	Responses to a satisfaction questionnaire (7-category Likert scale) by parents and representatives of referral agencies	Listing of average rating by year; calculation of percentage of questionnaires with rating of 6 or 7 by independent raters.	32 (parents) 35 (referral agencies)	100% 100%
	Verbal and written responses to an 8-item (+ or -) satisfaction questionnaire by Board of Trustee members.	Calculation of the average number marked + divided by the total number of items X 100% by independent raters.	20 (6 verbal reports FY 1978, 14 verbal/ written reports in FY 1983)	100%

71% to 100% with an average reliability score of 97.7% across the 16 dependent measures. It should also be noted that reliability checks were regularly made of all data collected in the course of conducting behavior change projects for the program's clients.

RESULTS

Table 3 presents a summary of data indicating the effectiveness of the institutional change strategies implemented in the present study. In general, a comparison of data recorded prior to (FY 1978), and following (FY 1983), the implementation of institutional change strategies revealed that virtually every aspect of program operation was positively affected.

Table 3

Summary of Data Indicating the Effects

of Institutional Change[1]

			FY 1978	FY 1983
A.	Funding			
	1.	Annual operating budget (excluding grant funding):	$604,655	$1,707,846
	2.	Number of grants received during previous five-year period:	4	18
	3.	Grant revenue during previous five-year period:	$18,000	$630,000

Table 3, continued

4.	Average (mean) program cost quotient for previous three-year period (excluding grant funding):[2]	$184,229	$172,559
B.	**Staffing**		
1.	Number of personnel (FTE):	60	88
2.	Staff turnover:	90%	27%
3.	Interns and practicum students in training at Institute:	0	12
C.	**Service Delivery**		
1.	Number of clients served: (average monthly census)	37.5	42.7
2.	Average level of staff-to-client interaction:[3]	40%	84%
3.	Degree to which program's services have been moved to community:[4]	0	32%
4.	Number of clients receiving psychotropic medication:	8	0
5.	Total number of clients discharged during previous four-year period:	18	34
6.	Average (mean) length of stay for clients discharged during three-year period:	7.1 years	4.2 years
7.	Percentage of those discharged who returned to natural home or foster home:	19%	57%
8.	Percentage of clients discharged to home or foster homes who required no further residential treatment:	0	96%
d.	**Public Relations and Professional Activity**		
1.	University affiliations (formal affiliations for the purpose of training graduate and undergraduate interns and practicum students):	0	13
2.	Conference and convention presentations by program staff during previous five years:	3	217
3.	Publications (books, chapters, articles) by program staff during previous five years (published, in press, or under contract):	0	57
4.	Consumer satisfaction: a. Percentage of parents reporting satisfaction with the program's staff and services:	N/A	85%
	b. Percentage of referral agencies reporting satisfaction with the program's staff and services:	N/A	87%

Table 3, continued

c. Percentage of Board
of Trustee membership
reporting satisfaction
with overall program
operation: 0   100%

[1]Data included in this table were obtained from rating forms and
written records which were carefully checked to ensure their reliability. Interrater reliability ranged from 71% to 100% with an
average of 97.7% (see Table 2).

[2]Program cost quotient = Annual operating budget divided by client
census (monthly average for the year), multiplied by average (mean)
length of stay for clients discharged.

[3]Pla-check rating (Doke & Risley, 1972) indicating average percentage of clients actively interacting with staff or involved in
the completion of some assigned task when randomly observed over a
period of several days.

[4]Percentage of Institute personnel (FTE) working off-grounds in
community-based classroom, vocational training, communication training, and parent training programs.

N/A - No data available; no comparison possible

Funding

As indicated in Figure 3, during the five year period of institutional change, the program's operating revenue (excluding grant
funding) increased by well over 100%, despite the fact that cost of
living increments in the program's budget, as allowed by its state's
Rate Setting Commission, would have resulted in an increase in
operating revenue of only about 63% during this period. The
balance of the increased operating revenue was obtained by securing
the support of funding agencies for program improvement through
the process of rate adjustment.

Despite this growth in funding, the cost effectiveness of the program's services increased during the period of institutional change.
Figure 4 presents these data in terms of "program cost quotients"
obtained by completing the following calculation for each fiscal
year: ([Annual operating budget controlled for inflation] ÷ [Aver-
age monthly client census]) × (Average length of stay for clients
discharged). This formula yielded a figure that represented the cost
effectiveness of services provided during each fiscal year. As indicated in Figure 4, the average (mean) cost quotient for FY
1976-1978 was $184,229 as compared to $167,798 for FY
1979-1983, representing a decrease of 10%. While this difference is
not dramatic, it suggests that the cost of institutional change was
reasonable given the impressive results obtained.

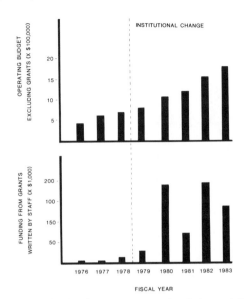

FIGURE 3. Total funding for program operation during each fiscal year.

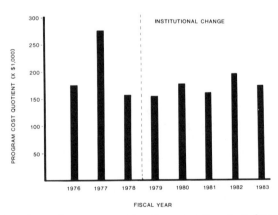

FIGURE 4. Annual cost of program operation. Program cost quotients for each fiscal year were calculated by dividing the program's annual operating budget by its average client census for the year and multiplying the resulting figure by the average length of stay for clients discharged from the program during the year. Decreasing cost quotients indicate increasing cost effectiveness.

In addition, a survey of other Massachusetts human service programs conducted in 1982, supplemented by information obtained from the Massachusetts Rate Setting Commission and the Massachusetts Departments of Education and Social Services, indicated that the program reportedly had the *lowest annual tuition rate* (annual costs per client of $37,943), the *shortest length of stay* for clients served (mean of two years, 11 months), and the *lowest rate of recidivism* (only one client of 22 discharged to their homes or foster homes required further residential treatment) relative to other residential educational programs specializing in the treatment of autistic youth. Specifically, the cost (annual tuition rate) of the Institute's services in FY 1983 was an average of 24% (range of 1% to 55%) less than the costs of other residential educational programs for autistic children in Massachusetts and other neighboring states.

As also indicated in Figure 3, grant revenue increased dramatically, enabling the Institute to (1) completely renovate its physical plant; (2) conduct applied research and demonstration projects that would lead to the establishment of permanent operating budget support for service programs such as outreach parent training/in-home consultation, group home programming, and vocational training; (3) purchase vehicles for transporting children to and from community-based activities (e.g., playgrounds, schools, libraries, etc.); (4) construct a community-based group home; and (5) employ additional personnel to assist in training, evaluation, and research activities.

Staffing

Increased fund raising as well as improved personnel recruitment, training, supervision, and administrative structure enabled the Institute to develop a larger, more qualified work force. As indicated in Figure 5, the staff employed (FTE) in FY 1983 was 45% larger than that employed in FY 1978, despite the fact that the average client census increased by only 13% during the same period. In addition, the 1983 work force included a greater percentage of college graduates and individuals holding postgraduate degrees. Specifically, the 1983 work force included five PhD behavioral psychologists with an average of five years postdoctoral experience (as opposed to one PhD in 1978). Similarly, over 95% of the direct service and support service staff employed in 1983 were college graduates (as opposed to less than 75% in 1978).

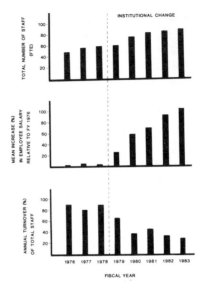

FIGURE 5. Total number (full time equivalent), average annual increase in salary (relative to FY 1976 salary levels), and average annual turnover (total number leaving employment—total FTE) for staff employed by the program during each fiscal year.

Staff turnover decreased dramatically from over 90% in FY 1978 to less than 30% in FY 1983. The average salary for direct service staff increased more than 100% from FY 1976 to FY 1983, representing an increase significantly higher than the rate of inflation for the period (63% based on inflation factors utilized by the Massachusetts Rate Setting Commission). Benefits for staff also increased by more than 100%.

There was also evidence that, following institutional change, program staff exhibited a number of behaviors characteristic of a professional work force. By the end of the second year of institutional change, each client was being served by a well-trained case manager who coordinated the day-to-day treatment planning and programming for the client and who completed an average of between 12 and 15 data-based behavior change projects for the client each year. (Prior to institutional change, no data-based behavior change projects were initiated.) As shown in Figure 6, staff also became more involved in applied research and related professional activity (e.g., attending professional conferences, planning for graduate education, publication, etc.) as can be seen in the number of publications (57) and conference presentations (217) by program staff during the course of institutional change (Blew, Williams, & Christian, 1982).

Service Delivery

Institutional change had the effect of greatly improving both the quantity and quality of services to clients. New service programs were initiated (e.g., parent training, community-based group home, in-home consultation, transitional programming, vocational training) and existing programs were improved (e.g., educational and residential services, communication training). The more progressive, comprehensive aspect of service programming can be seen in Figure 7 which indicates that the program's clients no longer required the use of "chemical restraint" (psychotropic medication) for the control of their behavior.

Services to clients also became more individualized and intensive as indicated by an increase in the level of staff-to-client therapeutic interaction of more than 100% (see Table 3). The "quality" of staff to client interaction also changed, in that more emphasis was placed on the "criterion of ultimate functioning" (Brown, Nietupski, & Hamre-Nietupski, 1976) in service planning and programming

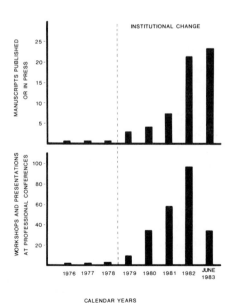

FIGURE 6. Total number of manuscripts published (in press) and workshop/conference presentations made by program staff each calendar year through May, 1983.

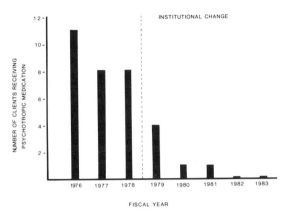

FIGURE 7. Total number of program clients receiving psychotropic medication as of July 1 of each fiscal year.

(Dyer, Schwartz, & Luce, 1982). Specifically, programming was guided by a determination of where the client eventually would be living so that he or she could be taught the skills that would facilitate such a transition. In addition, more attention was given to the teaching of community living skills and to the utilization of incidental teaching strategies (Hart & Risley, 1982), since this type of programming has been shown to increase the probability that skills acquired are likely to be used and maintained.

Similarly, on-grounds living units were renovated and remodeled to more closely approximate a home environment; a community-based group home was constructed; classrooms were moved off-grounds to a vacated public school facility which also housed a collaborative Head Start Program; and a variety of new community-based training programs were initiated. For example, in 1982 and 1983, programs were designed and implemented to teach autistic clients to play with their normal peers in the community (Blew, McGrale, Schwartz, Olson, & Gruber, 1982); to exhibit basic safety skills such as pedestrian crossing; and to manage money and exhibit appropriate grocery shopping skills (McGrale, Butler, & Rotholz, 1982). Furthermore, by January, 1983, almost one-third (32%) of the Institute's services had been moved off-grounds to the community (i.e., 32% of the Institute's direct service personnel were working off-grounds in community-based classroom and group-home settings).

It is not surprising, therefore, that the average length of stay for clients discharged from the program decreased from an average of 7 years, 1 month (3 years, 7 months for clients served) in FY 1976-1978 to an average of 4 years, 7 months (3 years, 4 months for clients served) in FY 1979-1983. Most importantly, the number of clients discharged from the program increased by over 100%, from 15 in FY 1976-1978 to 37 in FY 1979-1983. In addition, the percentage of clients discharged who returned to their homes or foster homes increased from an average of 19% for FY 1976-1978 to 57% for FY 1979-1983. Furthermore, 21 of the 22 clients (95%) discharged to their homes or foster homes during the period of institutional change required no further residential treatment of any kind (i.e., no return to the program and no admission to another residential program).

Legal Safety

During the five-year period of institutional change, the following

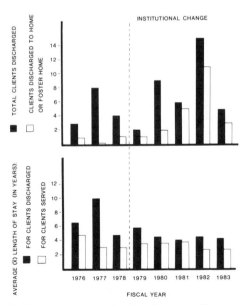

FIGURE 8. Length of stay and discharge data for clients served by the program. Length of stay for clients discharged was calculated by determining the difference between the admission and discharge dates for clients discharged during each fiscal year and computing a yearly average (mean). Length of stay for clients served was calculated by determining the difference between admission dates and June 1 of each fiscal year and computing a yearly average (mean).

legal safeguards were established or implemented: (1) Parent Advisory Board, Professional Advisory Board, and Human Rights Committee to provide an ongoing review of program operation and to ensure that the treatment procedures used by program staff were appropriate and effective; (2) an overall framework for program evaluation and quality assurance; (3) forms and procedures effective in safeguarding clients' rights to informed consent and confidentiality; (4) orientation and training for program staff in issues and strategies pertinent to legal safety; and (5) effective case record review and client tracking systems. (*None* of these safeguards was either planned or implemented prior to the initiation of institutional change.) Furthermore, an on-site review of the program by its Human Rights Committee in June, 1982, indicated (100% agreement) that every aspect of program operation (e.g., physical plant, service programs, and staff performance) was "appropriate to the age, functioning level, and special needs of the program's clients."

Public Relations

Feedback obtained from the program's consumers (parents/legal guardians), funding/referral agencies (social service agencies and school districts), Professional Advisory Board members, Parent Advisory Board members, affiliated universities, and members of the Board of Trustees has indicated that the program is generally considered to be reputable and highly effective. Satisfaction questionnaires (7 category Likert scale) completed in FY 1983 by consumers, funding/referral agencies, and members of the Board of Trustees indicated a high level of satisfaction with the program's staff as well as its services. Specifically, 32 of 41 parents completed and returned questionnaires; 85.6% of the responses indicated complete satisfaction/satisfaction with program services, 84.3% indicated complete satisfaction/satisfaction with program staff. Similarly, 35 of 50 representatives from social service/funding agencies completed and returned questionnaires; 81.7% indicated complete satisfaction/satisfaction with program services, 92.9% indicated complete satisfaction/satisfaction with program staff.

Feedback obtained from each of these sources also has indicated that the program had "greatly improved" (both staff and services) since 1978. It is not surprising, therefore, that the number of client referrals for the program's services increased by over 500% in FY 1982 relative to FY 1978.

DISCUSSION

The present case study utilized an approach to institutional change characterized by a well-planned and coordinated sequence of operations including: (1) Developing plans and goals for change; (2) establishing functional organizational structure; (3) recruiting, orienting, and training management and direct service personnel; (4) contracting for staff performance; (5) scheduling, supervising, and evaluating personnel; (6) obtaining and managing financial resources; (7) evaluating program operation; (8) promoting positive public relations; (9) ensuring legal safety; and (1) disseminating results. When these procedures were applied in an institutional human service setting, every aspect of program operation (e.g., organizational structure, personnel management, service delivery, legal safety, funding, and public relations) was significantly modified.

Results indicated that procedures similar to those developed by behavioral researchers in human service settings can be packaged and systematically implemented to initiate and maintain institutional change. These procedures include (1) planning for behavioral change (Luthans & Krietner, 1975); (2) behavioral orientation and training of human service personnel (Christian & Troy, 1983; Faw, Reid, Schepis, Fitzgerald, & Welty, 1981; Montegar, Reid, Madsen, & Ewell, 1977; Page, Christian, Iwata, Reid, Crow, & Dorsey, 1981; Page, Iwata, & Reid, 1982); (3) performance contracting (Christian, 1981b, 1982a); (4) behavioral supervision (Ivancic, Reid, Iwata, Faw, & Page, 1981; Montegar et al., 1977; Quiltich, 1975; Reid & Shoemaker, in press); (5) program evaluation (Christian, 1981b; Doke & Risley, 1972); (6) consultation and peer review (Christian, 1983a, 1983b); and (7) behavioral treatment of autistic children (Koegel, Russo, & Rincover, 1977; Luce & Christian, 1981).

Despite the impressive results of this study, there remain questions concerning the relative effectiveness of the specific procedures utilized in promoting institutional change. In the absence of an analysis of the individual components utilized in this packaged approach, it is difficult to determine whether one component was more important or effective than another. Additional research in the area of component analysis may make it possible to emphasize certain components of the approach and/or deemphasize or eliminate others to accomplish institutional change more efficiently and/or cost effectively.

Another question concerns the probability that this approach to institutional change can be successfully replicated in other human service settings (i.e., programs with different needs and resources, client populations, funding sources, staffing, etc.). In this regard, it is important to identify aspects of the setting in the present study that may make such replication difficult. For example, the study was conducted at a private, non-profit program that was able to qualify as a tax-exempt corporation and receive grants from philanthropic foundations. In addition, the program was smaller, less bureaucratic, and allowed more flexible budgeting practices than the typical state institution. The program was also located in a resort area which facilitated recruitment of staff and possibly helped contribute to low staff turnover. Furthermore, the program served autistic clients, who require more expert, intensive staffing than clients with less-severe handicapping conditions. This provided the program with the rationale and justification for developing improved staff-to-client ratios, increasing the level of staff expertise, introducing PhD-level supervisory personnel, and utilizing individualized, data-based treatment methods.

Finally, and most importantly, replication of this study will be difficult in any setting that does not permit the implementation of a top-down approach to institutional change. In the present study, a supportive governing board entrusted the direction and management of the program to a behavioral psychologist who served as the program's chief administrator. Replication will be difficult in situations lacking a supportive board or supervisory state officials as well as in situations where a sufficiently autonomous executive director lacks the management and program development skills necessary to implement the strategies that have been described.

Because of these potential obstacles to replication, efforts have been made to package the strategies employed at the May Institute in such a way as to provide a systematic "how to" approach to human service programming and management. In addition to this article, a series of books have been published describing management methods (Christian & Hannah, 1983), programming models (Christian, Hannah, & Glahn, in press), treatment procedures (Luce & Christian, 1981), and legal safety strategies (Hannah et al., 1981). An extensive bibliography of all research conducted at the Institute (Blew et al., 1982) and policy and procedure manuals for key components of the program (e.g., performance contracting; case manager system; data collection and analysis; orientation and training; program evaluation) have been developed. In 57 publications and 217 presentations (see Figure 6) since FY 1978, Institute staff have attempted to systematically evaluate and package all of the procedures considered important to a successful replication of its program. In this way, it is hoped that the program will be more dependent upon the technology it has developed than on the expertise and ingenuity of the staff it has employed.

In addition, despite the unique aspects of the program that may make replication difficult, it is important to note the following: (1) The program in the present study displayed many characteristics of the ineffective, custodial institutions described in the literature (e.g., Risley & Favell, 1979); (2) the procedures utilized in the study are extensions of those reported in the research literature on applied behavior analysis and organizational behavior management (e.g., Kazdin, 1980; Luthans & Kreitner, 1975; Miller, 1978); (3) virtually every area of program operation was affected by the study (see Table 3); and (4) institutional change resulting from the study has proven durable over time, despite ongoing changes in the program's personnel and client population (see Figures 3-8).

Within the limitations imposed by case study design (Johnston & Pennypacker, 1980; Kazdin, 1973), the results of this investigation suggest that institutional change is possible and that the technology required to effect such change is currently available. As behaviorists in human service settings focus more of their attention on this problem, more effective, efficient models and methods for institutional change are sure to be developed. As improved administrative systems, organizational models, and management methods become available, they must be effectively disseminated to those responsible for the development, financial support, supervision, and evaluation of human service programs. State departments of education and human services can play pivotal roles in this effort, by identifying institutional change as a priority and providing resources and support necessary to promote change in public as well as private human service programs.

NOTES

1. Additional information concerning this type of organizational structure, and how special projects within such a structure can be planned and managed, is provided by Christian and Hannah (1983).
2. Adapted from Christian (1981b).
3. Adapted from Christian and Hannah (1983).
4. *Ibid.*

REFERENCES

American Psychological Association. (1977). *Ethical Standards of Psychologists: 1977 Revision.* Washington, D.C.: American Psychological Association.

Anderson, S. R., Luce, S. C., Newsom, C. D., Gruber, B. K., & Butler, K. K. (1982). *Individualized treatment planning for Autistic Youth.* Paper presented at the Annual Convention of the Association for Advancement of Behavior Therapy, Los Angeles.

Anderson, S. R., McGrale, J. E., Norris, M. B., Luce, S. C., and Christian, W. P. (1982). *Transition of autistic children to less restrictive environments: A model treatment project.* Paper presented at the Annual Convention of the Association for Advancement of Behavior Therapy, Los Angeles.

Andrasik, F., & McNamara, J. R. (1977). Optimizing staff performance in an Institutional Behavior Change System: A pilot study. *Behavior Modication, 1,* 235-248.

Association for the Advancement of Behavior Therapy. (1978). *Ethical issues for human services.* New York: Association for Advancement of Behavior Therapy.

Balthazar, E. (1972). Residential programs in adaptive behavior for the emotionally disturbed and mentally retarded. *Mental Retardation, 10,* 10-13.

Blew, P. A., Luce, S. C., & Christian, W. P. (1982). *Effective strategies for disseminating behavior analysis and therapy.* Paper presented at the Annual Convention of the Association for Advancement of Behavior Therapy, Los Angeles.

Blew, P. A., McGrale, J. E., Schwartz, I., Olson, J. M., & Gruber, B. K. (1982). *Developing interaction skills of autistic children using normal children as teachers.* Paper presented at the Annual Convention for Behavior Analysis, Milwaukee.

Blew, P. A., Williams, M. E., & Christian, W. P. (1982). A bibliography of presentations and publications by the staff of the May Institute. *May Institute Research Bulletin, 1*(1), 1-27.

Brown, L., Nietupski, J., & Hamre-Nietupski, S. (1976). The criterion of ultimate functioning and public school services for severely handicapped students. In L. Brown, N. Certo, K. Belmore, & T. Crowner (Eds.), *Papers and programs related to public school services for secondary age severely handicapped students.* Vol. VI, Part I. Madison, WI: Madison Metropolitan School District.

Christian, W. P. (1981a). Behavioral administration of the residential treatment program. *The Behavior Therapist, 4*(1), 3-6.

Christian, W. P. (1981b). Programming quality assurance in the residential rehabilitation setting: A model for administrative work performance standards. *Journal of Rehabilitation Administration, 5*(1), 26-33.

Christian, W. P. (1981c). The biannual report: A model for structuring human service program evaluation and dissemination. *Journal of Rehabilitation Administration, 5*(3), 108-115.

Christian, W. P. (1981d). Reaching autistic children: Strategies for parents and helping professionals. In A. Milunsky (Ed.) *Coping with crisis and handicap.* New York: Plenum Press, pp. 231-246.

Christian, W.P. (1982a). Work performance contracting: An essential feature of accountable human service administration. *Journal of Mental Health Administration, 9*(2), 39-42.

Christian, W. P. (1982b). How to obtain foundation grants for behavioral research and program development. *The Behavior Therapist, 5*(4), 129-133.

Christian, W. P. (1983a). Managing the performance of the human service consultant. *The Behavior Therapist, 6,* 47-49.

Christian, W. P. (1983b). Professional peer review: Recommended strategies for reviewer and reviewee. *The Behavior Therapist, 6,* 86-89.

Christian, W. P. (in press a). The effects of institutional change. In W. P. Christian, G. T. Hannah, & T. J. Glahn (Eds.), *Programming effective human services: Strategies for institutional change and client transition.* New York: Plenum Press.

Christian, W. P. (in press b). Ensuring legal safety in mental health programming: Critical issues and effective strategies. *Administration in Mental Health.*

Christian, W. P. & Hannah, G. T. (1983). *Effective management in human services.* Englewood Cliffs, New Jersey: Prentice-Hall.

Christian, W. P., Hannah, G. T., & Glahn, T. J. (Eds.). (in press). *Programming effective human services: Strategies for institutional change and client transition.* New York: Plenum Press.

Christian, W. P., & Troy, P. J. (1983). A comparison of methods for orienting new personnel to the human service setting. *Journal of Mental Health Administration 10*(2), 49-51.

Czyzewski, M. J., Christian, W. P., & Norris, M. B. (in press). Preparing the family for client transition: Outreach parent training. In W. P. Christian, G. T. Hannah, and T. J. Glahn (Eds.). *Programming effective human services: Strategies for institutional change and client transition.* New York: Plenum Press.

Doke, L. A., & Risley, T. R. (1972). The organization of day care environments: Required vs. optional activities. *Journal of Applied Behavior Analysis, 5,* 405-420.

Dyer, K., Schwartz, I. S., & Luce, S. C. (1982). *Improving the quality of planned activities through staff feedback.* Paper presented at the Annual Convention of the Association for Behavior Analysis, Milwaukee.

Faw, G. D., Reid, D. H., Schepis, M. M., Fitzgerald, J. R., & Welty, P. A. (1981). Involving institutional staff in the development and maintenance of sign language skills with profoundly retarded persons. *Journal of Applied Behavior Analysis, 14,* 411-423.

Glahn, T. J., & Christian, W. P. (1982). *Staff exchange programs: A vehicle for increasing staff knowledge and motivation.* Paper presented at the Annual Convention of the Association for the Advancement of Behavior Therapy, Los Angeles.

Gray, J. L. (1974). Matrix organization design as a vehicle for effective delivery of public health care and social services. *Management International Review, 11,* 73-82.

Hall, R. V. (1975). *Managing behavior.* (Part I-IV). Lawrence, Kansas: H&H Enterprises.

Hannah, G. T., Christian, W. P., & Clark, H. B. (Eds.). (1981). *Preservation of client rights: A handbook for practitioners providing therapeutic, educational and rehabilitative services.* New York: Macmillan/Free Press.

Hart, B. M., & Risley, T. R. (1982). *How to use incidental teaching for elaborating language.* Lawrence, Kansas: H&H Enterprises, Inc.

Hersen, M., & Bellack, A. S. (1978a). Staff training and consultation. In M. Hersen & A. S. Bellack (Eds.). *Behavior therapy in the psychiatric setting.* Baltimore: Williams & Wilkins, pp. 58-87.

Hersen, M., & Bellack, A. S. (Eds.). (1978b). *Behavior therapy in the psychiatric setting.* Baltimore: Williams & Wilkins.

Horner, D. R. (1980). The effects of an environmental "enrichment" program on the behavior of institutionalized profoundly retarded children. *Journal of Applied Behavior Analysis, 13,* 473-491.

Ivancic, M. T., Reid, D. H., Iwata, B. A., Faw, G. D., & Page, T. J. (1981). Evaluating a supervision program for developing and maintaining therapeutic staff-resident interactions during institutional care routines. *Journal of Applied Behavior Analysis, 14,* 95-107.

Johnston, J. M., & Pennypacker, H. S. (1980). *Strategies and tactics of human behavioral research.* Hillsdale, New Jersey: Lawrence Erlbaum Associates.

Kazdin, A. E. (1973). Methodological and assessment considerations in evaluating reinforcement programs in applied settings. *Journal of Applied Behavior Analysis, 6,* 517-531.

Kazdin, A. E. (1979). Advances in child behavior therapy: Applications and implications. *American Psychologist, 34*(10), 981-987.

Kazdin, A. E. (1980). *Behavior modification in applied settings.* (Revised Ed.) Homewood, Ill: The Dorsey Press.

Joint Commission on Accreditation of Hospitals. (1978). *Standards for services of developmentally disabled individuals.* Chicago: Joint Commission on Accreditation of Hospitals.

Koegel, R. L., Russo, D. C., & Rincover, A. (1977). Assessing and training teachers in the generalized use of behavior modification with autistic children. *Journal of Applied Behavior Analysis, 10,* 197-205.

Krapfl, J. (1982). Behavior management in state mental health systems. *Journal of Organizational Behavior Management, 3*(3), 91-105.

Luce, S. C., Blew, P. A., & Thibadeau, S. F. (1983). *Research and dissemination strategies for the human service program.* Paper presented at the Annual Convention of the Association for Behavior Analysis. Milwaukee.

Luce, S. C., & Christian, W. P. (Eds.). (1981). *How to work with autistic and severely handicapped youth: A series of eight training manuals.* Lawrence, Kansas: H&H Enterprises.

Luce, S. C., Anderson, S. R., Thibadeau, S. F., & Lipsker, L. E. (in press). Preparing the client for transition to the community. In W. P. Christian, G. T. Hannah, & T. J. Glahn (Eds.). *Programming effective human services: Strategies for institutional change and client transition.* New York: Plenum Press.

McGrale, J., Butler, K. K., & Rotholz, D. (1982). *Independent shopping by autistic children.* Paper presented at the Annual Convention of the Association for the Advancement of Behavior Therapy, Los Angeles.

Miller, L. M. (1978). *Behavioral management: The new science of managing people at work.* New York: John Wiley & Sons.

Montegar, C. A., Reid, D. H., Madsen, C. H., & Ewell, M. D. (1977). Increasing institutional staff-to-resident interactions through inservice training and supervisor approval. *Behavior Therapy, 8,* 533-540.

Nihira, K., Foster, R., Shellhaas, M., & Leland, H. (1974). *AAMD Adaptive Behavior Scale* (Rev. Ed.). Washington, D.C.: American Association on Mental Deficiency.

Page, T. J., Christian, J. G., Iwata, B. A., Reid, D. H., Crow, R. E., & Dorsey, M. F. (1981). Evaluating and training interdisciplinary teams in writing IPP goals and objectives. *Mental Retardation, 19,* 25-27.

Page, T. J., Iwata, B. A., & Reid, D. H. (1982). Pyramidal training: A large-scale application with institutional staff. *Journal of Applied Behavior Analysis, 15,* 335-351.

Quilitch, H. R. (1975). A comparison of three staff-management procedures. *Journal of Applied Behavior Analysis, 8*(1), 59-66.

Reid, D. H., & Shoemaker, J. (in press). Behavioral supervision: Methods of improving institutional staff performance. In W. P. Christian, G. T. Hannah, & T. J. Glahn (Eds.) *Programming effective human services: Strategies for institutional change and client transition.* New York: Plenum Press.

Reppucci, N. D. (1977). Implementation issues for the behavior modifier as institutional change agent. *Behavior Therapy, 8,* 594-605.

Reppucci, N. D., & Saunders, J. T. (1974). Social psychology and behavior modification: Problems of implementation in natural settings. *American Psychologist, 2*(9), 649-660.

Risley, T. R., & Favell, J. E. (1979). Constructing a living environment in an institution. In L. A. Hamerlynck (Ed.), *Behavioral systems for the developmentally disabled: II. Institutional, clinic, and community environments.* New York: Brunner/Mazel, pp. 3-24.

Ritvo, E. R., & Freeman, B. J. (1977). National Society for Autistic Children definition of the syndrome of autism. *Journal of Pediatric Psychology, 2*(4), 146.

Rotholz, D., Newsom, D. D., Luce, S. C., & Christian, W. P. (1982). *Teaching human service staff to prompt management for reinforcement.* Paper presented at the Annual Convention of the Association for Behavior Analysis, Milwaukee.

Tharp, R., & Wetzel, R. (1969). *Behavior modification in the natural environment.* New York: Academic Press.

Thibadeau, S. F., Butler, K. K., Gruber, B. K., Luce, S. C., Newsom, C. D. Anderson, S. R., & Christian, W. P. (1982). *Competency-based orientation and training of human service personnel.* Paper presented at the Annual Convention of the Association for the Advancement of Behavior Therapy, Los Angeles.

Thompson, T., & Grabowski, J. (Eds.). (1972). *Behavior modification of the mentally retarded.* New York: Oxford University Press.

Wedel, K. R. (1976). Matrix design for human service organizations. *Administration in Mental Health, 4*, 36-42.

Wyatt v. Stickney, 325 F. Suppl. 781, *aff'd on rehearing*, 344 F. Supp. 1341 (M.C. Ala. 1971), *aff'd on rehearing* 344 F. Supp. 373, *aff'd in separate decision*, 344 F. Supp. 387 (M.D. Ala. 1972), aff'd sub nom, Wyatt V. Aderholt, 503 F.2d 1305 (5th Cir. 1974).

Changing Patterns of Residential Care: A Case Study of Administrative and Program Changes

Craig C. Jensen
Patricia Morgan
Richard Orduño
Marcy A. Self
Reuben G. Zarate
Gary Meunch
David Peck
Robert A. Reguera
Bernard Shanley

ABSTRACT. The use of soft-tie restraint, a common means of controlling the assaultive behavior of mentally retarded residents in institutions, was examined with a retrospective design. Naturally occurring changes over a 39-month period were divided into (a) changes in management personnel that were associated with changes in management support of behavioral programming, (b) changes in staff training and feedback, and (c) a change in the physical location of the Program. Use of restraint decreased when the use of behavioral programming was supported by management and increased when it was not. When a four-person Training Team provided staff with training and formal and informal feedback, restraint was used less than it was when the Training Team was outside the Program and training and feedback were not provided. Changing the physical

The authors wish to thank Simma Siskind, RN, Psychiatric Nursing Education Director at Sonoma State Developmental Center, who is responsible for the creation of the Sonoma Developmental Training Team, and those staff whose cooperation and hard work made possible the reductions in the use of restraint reported here. We also wish to thank Keri Procunier, Executive Director at Agnews State Hospital, who provided strong support for the activities of the two Training Teams and the management staff in the Program. Helpful comments by Dr. Daniel Fallon on an earlier version of this paper are also greatly appreciated. Appreciation is also expressed to two anonymous reviewers whose comments made important revisions possible. Remaining deficiencies are the sole responsibility of the authors. Reprints may be obtained from Craig C. Jensen, who is now at PAT 5, Fircrest School, 15230 15th Avenue N.E., Seattle, WA 98155.

location of the Program had little effect on the use of restraint. Relative to baseline, use of restraint decreased by 80% when management supported the use of behavioral programming and the Training Team was in the Program providing training and feedback. Reductions in the use of restraint were correlated with a corresponding reduction in Special Incident Reports which were filed when an event such as injury to a resident or staff member occurred.

In the past two decades behavioral techniques have been successfully applied to a wide range of behavioral problems exhibited by people who are mentally retarded. Although behavioral approaches are effective in ameliorating many of the problems exhibited by these people, there is a wide discrepancy between the success of programs reported in the literature and those actually implemented in institutions (Balthazar, 1972; Liberman, 1979). The gulf that exists between the power of available service technology and the limited successes of actual institutional programs emphasizes the importance of developing effective adminstrative methods in the area of delivery of services.

Risley and Favell (1979) have described the inadequacies of most institutions designed to serve the mentally retarded and these inadequacies are no doubt important factors in poor delivery of services. These problems normally include, but are not limited to, the following: direct-service staff are often those who, for various reasons, can not find work elsewhere; direct-service staff rarely have previous training in areas relevant to their assignments; high rates of staff turnover yield a staff that is always relatively inexperienced; staff are poorly supervised; there is little or no positive feedback to staff for positive interactions with residents; instead, feedback is usually negative and in reaction to a crisis; and administrative structures are often only minimally related to the functional mode of operation of staff within the facility.

One solution to the problem of poor delivery of services that is often turned to by administrators of institutions for the mentally retarded is inservice training. Unfortunately, there is little research to justify faith in staff training by itself as a method for improving the behavior of direct-service staff and, consequently, the behavior of residents (Ziarnik & Bernstein, 1982). Typical inservice training classes consist primarily of lectures and readings away from the living unit of the residents and produce little more than an increased interest in behavior modification with little change in actual performance (Hall & Copeland, 1972; Gardner, 1972; Martin, 1972). In addition, inservice training in behavioral techniques typically emphasizes the application of these procedures on a individual basis even though direct-service staff are much more likely to find themselves working with groups of residents. Klaber (1969) objectively rated the services provided by six institutions for the mentally retarded and found that the least effective of them had the strongest inservice training programs. Overall there was no relationship between inservice training and how direct-service staff interacted with residents.

In a review of the effects of inservice training on staff performance, Ziarnik and Bernstein (1982) found no studies which show that inservice training by itself produces long-term changes in how staff interact with residents. As others (Favell, Risley, Wolfe, Riddle, & Rasmussen, 1981) conclude regarding individual training programs for the mentally retarded, this may simply mean that such programs are incorrectly applied: e.g., few inservice training programs make provision for actual implementation of newly acquired skills.

Ziarnik and Bernstein advocate using Organizational Behavior Management (OBM, Frederiksen & Lovett, 1980) procedures derived from operant psychology to improve staff performance and providing staff training only when specific skill deficits are identified. When relevant reinforcers such as pay, promotions, and days off have been used in systematic response-contingent programs with direct-service staff, application of behavioral techniques has uniformly improved (Iwata, Bailey, Brown, Foshee, & Alpern, 1976; Patterson, Griffin, & Panyan, 1976; Pomerleau, Bobrove, & Smith, 1973; Pommer & Streedbeck, 1974). Because of the difficulties involved in using these reinforcers, several studies have employed more easily implemented and less expensive written or graphic feedback of resident or staff behavior (Panyan, Boozer, & Morris, 1970; Quilitch, 1975; Welsch, Ludwig, Radiker, & Krapfl, 1973) or supervisor approval (Montegar, Reid, Madsen, & Ewell, 1977) and found that these procedures can also maintain the performance of staff.

Recent legal decisions may require agencies to not only provide direct-service staff with training in behavioral techniques, but also to assess the effectiveness of such training (Martin, 1975). The present study shows one way to prepare such an assessment retrospectively through the use of a time series analysis (Campbell & Stanley,

1966). The study presented here examines the results of naturally occurring changes that took place during 39 months of operation of a program designed to reduce or eliminate the severely assaultive behavior occurring among approximately 100 mentally retarded adolescents and adults. The measures that were analyzed are (1) hours in soft-tie restraint, (b) total number of different residents in restraint as a result of behavior that posed a danger to the resident himself or others, and (c) the total number of Special Incident Reports (SIR's) involving residents and staff. The results permit some tentative conclusions regarding the roles of, first, support by management of behavioral programs and, second, staff training and feedback in reducing severe behavior problems of residents in institutions for the mentally retarded.

The literature on procedures to improve staff performance in service delivery systems is limited. Furthermore, the existing research deals almost exclusively with the use of "narrow" variables such as feedback or supervisor approval to change the behavior of the lowest ranking employees in the organization. The present report deals with a broader variable, support by management of behavioral programming. Support by management has been informally observed to have major effects on the implementation of behavioral programs (e.g., Martin, 1972; Watson, 1976), but with the exception of a report by Pomerleau et al. (1973) this factor, because of ethical and other considerations, appears not to have been examined often on an experimental basis. In addition, the present study focuses on assessing the effectiveness of staff training and feedback on the implementation of a "least restrictive environment" in which severe behavior problems are handled with a minimum of physical restraint of the resident and with minimal restriction of his basic human rights. For variables such as these that have not been examined often on an experimental basis, retrospective designs can provide useful hypotheses regarding organizational issues where more rigorous designs might not be possible.

METHOD

Program and Setting

Of the approximately 950 residents of Agnews State Hospital in San Jose, California, in January, 1978, 133 were in the Behavior Adjustment Program. This program was designed for ambulatory adolescents and adults who have a wide variety of serious assaultive behaviors which prohibit placement in the community or inclusion in other programs at the facility. Although residents in the program represented the entire range of mental retardation, most of them were classified as severely and profoundly retarded and most of them were on maintenance dosages of psychotropic medication. The objective of the program was to eliminate or reduce serious assaultive behaviors so that residents could move to a less restrictive setting. The residents were distributed according to sex and func tioning levels among five living units, each containing a day hall and three dormitories. The program originally consisted of two units for females and three units for males. Through transfers to other programs and placements in the community or in other facilities, the population decreased enough to permit the closing of one unit in May, 1979. From June, 1979 through February, 1980, the Program had one co-educational unit and one unit for females and two units for males. From March, 1980 through March, 1981, the program had one unit for females and three units for males. At the time this study ended in March, 1981, the resident population in the program was 97.

One month after the beginning of this study in February, 1978, 115 direct-service staff were assigned to the five-unit program. Of the 115 direct-service staff, 97 (84%) worked on a full-time basis and 77 (67%) had Associate of Arts Degrees and licenses as Psychiatric Technicians. In March, 1981, staff assigned to the four-unit Program included 84 direct-service staff, with 58 of these (60%) working on a full-time basis and 50 (60%) having Associate of Arts degrees and licenses as Psychiatric Technicians. Excluding janitors, yearly staff turnover from December, 1978 to December, 1979, and from December, 1979 to December, 1980, was 50% and 53%, respectively, for direct-service staff and 53% and 50%, respectively, for off-unit staff. These yearly turnover rates are higher than the mean turnover rate (mean = 32.8%, standard deviation = 27.6%) found in a survey of public institutions by Lakin, Bruininks, Hill, and Hauber (1982).

Dependent Measures

Soft-tie restraint. When a resident became agitated enough to either injure others or himself, cloth ties were used to restrain him or her to a chair until the unit supervisor determined that he or she was calm. When in restraint, residents were checked every ½ hour to insure that they had proper blood circulation. The maximum time a resident remained in restraint at one time was 2 hours. The use of restraint was closely monitored by the physicians who authorized its use in writing and by Health Services Supervisors, registered nurses. In addition, facility policy required that each Program forward a monthly summary of the number of hours each resident was in soft-tie restraint to the Executive Director, the Clinical Director, the Director of Central Nursing Service, and the Chairperson of the Human Rights Committee (who was the senior author of this report). The restraint data for this report were taken from those summaries. The two measures of soft-tie restraint usage were the number of hours residents were in restraint and the number of different residents restrained per month.

Special Incident Reports (SIRs). SIRs were filed when an event occurred that was physically harmful to a resident or staff member or had the potential for adversely affecting the operation of the facility. In the majority of cases, SIRs were filed when a resident was absent from the facility without permission or when or she injured himself or herself, another resident, a staff member, or a member of the community. Reports of SIRs were initiated by the person discovering the incident and forwarded to the Program Director who, in turn, forwarded the original to the Clinical Director or Hospital Administrator. The Clinical Director or Hospital Administrator then forwarded the original to the Residents Rights Advocate who, if appropriate, forwarded it to the Medical Director or the Coordinator of Nursing Services. For this study, no attempt was made to break down SIRs into type of incident or to rank severity of each incident. Instead, the measure chosen was simply the number of SIRs reported each month.

Reliability. The reliability problems associated with using records of restraint usage and SIRs are similar to those found in other analyses of this type which, by their retrospective nature, preclude the possibility of having reliability observations made as the behavior occurs. At this institution this problem was minimized by having a variety of people participate in the authorization and monitoring of restraint usage and monitoring of SIRs. The order for restraint was given by the Physician for the unit, entered into the Physician's Orders, and signed by him or her. Direct-service staff were required to make a separate entry in the resident's chart describing the incident that preceded the use of restraint and the time that the resident was put into restraint. As previously mentioned, registered nurses closely monitored the use of restraint and monthly reports on restraint usage were sent to the Program Director, the Executive Director, the Clinical Director, the Coordinator of Nursing Services, and the Chairperson of the Human Rights Committee. Unauthorized or undocumented use of restraint or failure to report such lack of documentation was defined in facility policies as resident abuse. Facility policies required that such cases be investigated by the Special Investigator for the facility and confirmed cases resulted in termination of employment for those involved. In his role as Staff Psychologist and Director of the Agnews Developmental Training Team, the senior author of this report was present on the units almost daily, Monday through Friday during the 29 months of Phases 1 through 5 and never observed a resident in restraint without proper documentation. Therefore, even though the reliability of the data can not be examined through, for example, the comparison of different reports initiated by different staff members, it is likely that they are quite objective.

Design

The retrospective analysis was applied to seven distinct phases, or changes. They fall into three groups. The first group of changes contains three phases, all involving changes in informal policies and procedures that determine administrative support of behavioral programming: Team Process (Phase 1), New Executive Director (Phase 2), and New Program Director (Phase 3). The second group also contains three phases, all involving changes in staff training and feedback: Sonoma Training Team plus Maintenance (Phase 4), Agnews Training Team in Program (Phase 5), and Agnews Training Team outside Program (Phase 6). The last change involves a single phase, that of the physical location of the Program: Program Move (Phase 7). The three groups of changes can be considered as three separate experiments. The first three phases all involved changes in administrative support of behavioral programming, whereas the next three phases all involved changes in staff training and feedback which occurred in the absence of changes in administrative variables. The effects of the changed physical location can be evaluated by comparing the measures obtained after the move with those obtained prior to the move, but under the same management and staff training and feedback conditions.

Team process. The Executive Director of the facility during the Team Process phase was a behavioral psychologist who strongly supported behavioral programming by hiring a behavioral psychologist as Clinical Director who, in turn, hired two new behavioral psychologists. These two newly hired staff were the only Staff Psychologists assigned to the Behavior Adjustment Program. During this phase, the two Staff Psychologists concentrated on constructing a workable interdisciplinary team process to plan and implement habilitative programs for residents. Other areas requiring immediate attention at that time included developing and maintaining individual behavior modification programs for residents with the most severe behavior problems, updating all psychological evaluations, and developing criteria for entry and exit of residents to and from the Program.

New Executive Director. The Executive Director during the Team Process phase left in order to assume a new position as Director of the Department of Developmental Services. At the same time, the Clinical Director during the Team Process phase assumed a new position under the former Executive Director. After these departures, the two Staff Psychologists in the program did not initially have the strong support of the Executive Director of the facility. During this time, many of the formal and informal policies and procedures implemented during the previous phase which had provided strong support for behavioral programming were eliminated by the same program management staff that had previously supported and helped implement them.

New Program Director. The new Program Director, who was the former Assistant Program Director during the first two phases of the study, established as her priority the minimizing of resident and staff injuries in the program. As in Phase 1, program management again gave strong support to formal and informal policies and procedures designed to implement behavioral programming and this phase can, therefore, be considered as a partial return to the first phase. The new Program Director was especially supportive in the areas of development and maintenance of behavior modification programs for residents with severe behavior problems and also arranged for inservice behavior modification training for staff that resulted in the next phase.

Sonoma Training Team plus maintenance. The Developmental Training Team from Sonoma State Developmental Center which was composed of four Psychiatric Technicians, presented a week-long workshop to 20 staff in the Program. The training consisted of 24 hours of lectures and films, and 11 hours of applying techniques on a unit. Technical terms were kept to a minimum and the training primarily emphasized structuring the environment so that it would be possible to reinforce residents for compliance on tasks and self-help activities. Staff were taught to deal with disruptive behavior by preventing injury to residents and staff as impersonally as possible to minimize the reinforcement for such behavior. The use of soft tie restraint to prevent injury to residents and staff was already understood by most staff and instruction in this procedure was not given. The lecture on punishment emphasized how responses that the staff typically thought of as punishment probably reinforced residents for exhibiting maladaptive behavior. The only technique for directly reducing behavior that was taught to staff was contingent observation (Porterfield, Herbert-Jackson, & Risley, 1976). This was used without instructing the resident in the appropriate behavior. Instead, the resident was removed from the group as impersonally as possible and other residents were reinforced for an appropriate incompatible behavior. After the resident was calm, he or she was returned to the group and then reinforced for exhibiting the behavior modeled by the other residents. Timeout in a separate room was not allowed at the facility.

The training on the unit took place over three mornings from 6:30 to 8:30 a.m. which included the time at which the residents awoke in the morning through breakfast and from 12:00 to 1:00 p.m. which included lunch. During these times the Sonoma Training Team initially modeled behavioral techniques to use in working directly with individual residents and with groups of residents and then supervised the trainees as they applied the techniques.

Following training, a Staff Psychologist (the senior author of this report) attempted to maintain the recently learned skills of these staff by giving feedback to individual staff members on the unit and by publishing a monthly memorandum to all staff. This memorandum summarized the performance of each unit by noting decreases in hours of restraint or in the number of different residents restrained relative to the previous month and praised the collective staff on the unit where the reductions took place. Increases in either measure were not noted or commented on. Copies were sent to each unit and at the bottom of the last page it was noted that a copy was sent to the Executive Director and the Clinical Director of the facility. The memorandum also included a figure summarizing the two measures of restraint usage for the entire program.

Agnews Training Team in program. The Agnews State Hospital

Developmental Training Team began to present workshops based on the Sonoma model in September, 1979. The Agnews Training Team was composed of one Staff Psychologist, one Rehabilitation Therapist, and two direct-service Psychiatric Technicians who were the a.m. and p.m. Group Leaders in one of the dormitories of the unit where most of the staff participated in the original training and who, for seven months, had been using the techniques taught by the Sonoma Training Team. There were two major differences between the training offered by the Sonoma and Agnews Training Teams. The first was that the Sonoma Training Team presented lectures and involved trainees in work on the units throughout the week, whereas the Agnews Training Team devoted the first two days of training solely to lectures and the final three days to lectures and to training on the units. The second difference was that the training given on the units by the Agnews Training Team consisted solely of how to work with groups of residents since direct-service staff seldom were alone with a resident, but instead spent most of their working hours with groups of them.

As was done by the Sonoma Training Team, the Agnews Training Team initially modeled how to reinforce and ignore residents and then gradually had the trainees take over more of these activities until they were the only ones working directly with residents on the final day of training. From October, 1979, through May, 1980, the Agnews Training Team presented 10 workshops to 74 staff from the facility with a total of 66 staff coming from within the Program. All of the staff in the workshops normally worked directly with residents either as teachers or as direct-service staff.

The Agnews Training Team engaged in several activities designed to get the trainees to implement the skills they had learned. The Staff Psychologist continued to publish his monthly memo summarizing the use of restraint and, in addition, each morning at 8:30 a.m., the off-unit staff and the Unit Managers met to review the previous day's events and share information. Each Unit Manager gave his or her report for the previous day and the Training Team would applaud and indicate approval in a variety of ways for a report of no use of restraints on the previous day and would remain silent when this was not the case. For those staff who completed the training, the Agnews Training Team posted signs in their assigned work area to remind them of the main points of the workshop. The Training Team also helped each staff member who had been through training construct for each resident in his or her group a short list of behaviors to reinforce and ignore, and a list of reinforcers. Along with a daily activity schedule, all the signs were made with large print and were posted high on a wall near the area in the dormitory where direct-service staff spent most of their time with residents. In addition, the Training Team arranged to have individual pictures taken of each resident and these were posted next to each resident's respective lists of behaviors to reinforce and ignore and the list of reinforcers.

Agnews Training Team outside program. In this phase, the Agnews Training Team was taken out of the program to provide training to staff from the entire facility on a Program-by-Program and unit-by-unit basis. It was not possible to implement any ongoing staff monitoring and reinforcement systems prior to leaving and all feedback to staff from the Team including the monthly memorandum summarizing the use of restraint was discontinued.

Program move. To enable contractors to remodel, the physical location of the program was moved to another building.

RESULTS

Figure 1 presents the total number of hours that residents were in restraint over the 39-month period, with the vertical lines indicating the beginning and sometimes the end of various phases. The number of different residents in restraint each month is also presented in this figure. Figure 2 similarly presents the number of SIRs recorded each month. The major results are as follows:

- During the Team Process Phase, hours in restraint initially increased, but then showed an uninterrupted downward trend over the remaining 5 months of the phase.
- During the period of time between the appearance of the new Executive Director and the appearance of the new Program Director, hours in restraint increased from a total of 378 hours to 699 hours.
- In the first 3 months of the new Program Director's tenure, hours in restraint decreased from 724 to 370, a level approximating the one attained 6 months earlier when support for behavioral programming by program management was strong.
- After the Sonoma Training Team trained 20 staff in the program there was an immediate reduction in hours of restraint,

with all of the monthly totals during this phase being less than any of those during the preceding three phases.

- When the Agnews Training Team was training staff in the program and providing them with various types of feedback, hours in restraint again decreased with 5 of the 8 data points being lower than in any of the previous four phases of the study. This 8-month phase was associated with the least use of restraint during the study and relative to the first 5 months of Phase 1, hours in restraint were reduced by 80%.

- After the Agnews Training Team left the program, hours in restraint increased to a level similar to that obtained after the appearance of the Sonoma Training Team. Moving the program to another building had little effect on this level of restraint usage.

During the Phases 1-3, number of different residents in restraint remained relatively stable, suggesting that the large changes in hours of soft-tie restraint over this period of time resulted from

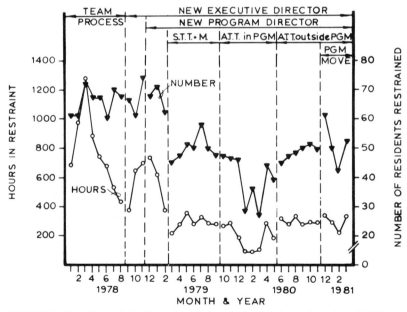

FIGURE 1. Monthly totals for hours in soft-tie restraint (circles) and number of different residents restrained (triangles) from January 1978, through March, 1981.

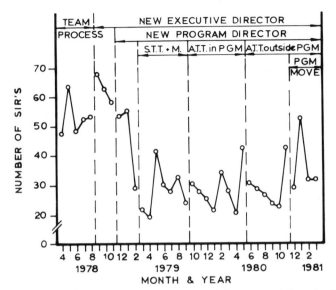

FIGURE 2. Total number of Special Incident Reports (SIRs) per month from April, 1978, through March, 1981.

changes in how long staff kept a resident in restraint once he was re-strained or how often each resident was restrained each month. The first sustained decrease in number of residents in restraint came im-mediately after the Sonoma Training Team presented their workshop. Over the 7 months of this phase, number of residents re-strained per month was lower than it had been in any of the three preceeding phases. When the Agnews Training Team was in the program, number of residents in restraint decreased again, with this measure during the last 5 months of this phase being at or below the lowest level achieved during all the preceeding phases. When the Agnews Training Team left the Program, number of residents in re-straint rose to a level comparable to that attained during Phase 4. Moving the Program to another building only produced an increase in the variability of the number of residents in restraint each month relative to the previous phase.

As Figure 2 shows, number of SIRs during Phase 1, like number of residents restrained, remained relatively constant despite the de-crease in hours of restraint. During Phase 2, when program man-agement did not strongly support behavioral programming, SIR's reached their highest level, while in Phases 4 through 6 they reached their lowest. Thus, the new Program Director was successful in meeting her goal of establishing a safer environment for residents and staff than was present prior to her tenure. The relatively low number of SIRs each month in Phases 4 through 6 indicates that the reductions in hours in restraint and number of residents in restraint during this period were not achieved by simply leaving residents unrestrained when they were dangerous to themselves or others.

Because the population decreased during the 39 months of the study from 133 residents to 97, this change provides an alternative explanation for the reductions in restraint usage and SIRs. Several factors make this explanation unlikely. First, as Figure 1 shows, the largest number of residents restrained in a month was 74, indicating that not all residents were assaultive enough to require this procedure. These less assaultive residents tended to be females and to be among the first transferred to other Programs or community facilities. Second, because the program was the only one at the institution that was designed to deal with assaultive behavior, there was no place to transfer residents who were highly assaultive. Third, the population decreased steadily throughout the study with the mean percentage decrease for each month being less than one per cent. The mean percentage decrease for each of the six phases relative to the previous phase was 4.1%, with the largest percentage decrease of this type being 7.7% and occurring in Phase 5. Despite this slow and steady decrease, relatively large changes in the restraint measures occurred in both directions and usually within two months following a change to a different phase. Finally, the closing of one unit in May, 1979 kept the population density on each unit at roughly the same level throughout the study. The largest number of residents per unit prior to this closing was 26.6 in January, 1978 and the lowest was 22.4 immediately prior to the closing in May, 1979. From the closing of this one unit to the conclusion of the study in March, 1981, the highest and lowest population density figures were 28.5 and 24.2, respectively.

DISCUSSION

The retrospective design of the present study correlated naturally occurring changes in (a) support by management of behavioral programming and (b) staff training and feedback with monthly values for the number of hours residents were restrained, the number of residents restrained, and the number of SIRs. The first three phases all involved changes in support from hospital management of behavioral programming, they clearly show that hours in restraint decreased when management personnel in the program supported the activities of those whose primary responsibility was the implementation of behavioral programs. When the management team no longer provided this support in the second phase of the study, hours in restraint increased and number of SIR's reached three of the four highest values recorded. Relative to the values obtained at the beginning of the study, the addition of staff training and feedback to support by management of behavioral programming led to large decreases in both measures of restraint use. In addition, the number of non-targeted SIRs decreased to the lowest levels observed in the study. This result occurred even though the Agnews Developmental Training Team did not attempt to reinforce staff for low numbers of SIR's and indicates that the training and feedback provided by this group affected not only use of restraint, but other non-targeted measures of program functioning as well.

As measured by both the use of restraint and number of SIRs, support by management of behavioral programming had a major impact on the overall functioning of the program. Although the role of management was essential in bringing about these reductions, they did not directly cause them. Instead, they created the conditions or, in operant terminology, ''set the occasion for'' other staff members in the Program to function more effectively and to engage in more behaviors related to improved habilitation programming for residents. The Program Director created these conditions in four ways. First, she initially set an explicit goal of creating a safer environment for residents and staff. Second, she provided verbal support for behavioral programming in meetings with staff at all levels in the organization, from direct-service staff to the Executive Director. Third, she listened to input regarding lack of skills in behavioral programming by most direct-service staff and provided some of the needed training through the Sonoma Developmental Training Team. Finally, she allocated the resources to create a Training Team within the Program to provide training and feedback. Without these behaviors on the part of the Program Director, it would have been difficult, if not impossible, to achieve the reductions in use of restraint and in number of SIRs reported here.

The other focus of the present study is on the role of staff training and feedback in determining how staff in institutional settings interact with residents. The results reported here permit no conclusions regarding the relative importance in this situation of training vs. feedback. Nevertheless, the large reductions in the use of restraint and the number of SIRs are consistent with Ziarnik and Bernstein's (1982) contention that OBM procedures need to be implemented more widely in institutional settings and that staff training alone should not be relied upon to produce changes in how staff interact with residents.

The Program Director in the present study had experience with behavioral techniques and was not hesitant to provide needed support for those who were supposed to implement these procedures. In other institutions and programs, behaviorally trained personnel may have to shape management staff in the implementation of more systematic behavioral programming. In these situations, performance feedback can be used as a tool in this process. Management personnel learn that with a retrospective study it costs little or nothing to objectively analyze measures that are clearly relevant to the goals of the Program. Using management's own data, it is then relatively easy to point out the advantages of various kinds of interventions. For example, in the present study, it would be possible to point out that relative to a baseline period from January through May, 1978, the changes in management and training during the subsequent 34 months permitted a monthly and yearly savings, respectively, of 577 and 6,924 hours in restraint and 14 and 168 fewer residents in restraint. Relative to a baseline from April through August, 1978, comparable savings for SIRs are 18 per month and 216 per year. Because SIRs are closely related to injuries to residents and staff and are associated with higher costs for disability insurance and time off from work and increase the probability of having a lawsuit filed against the facility, it should be possible with these data to shape management staff into supporting a complete system based on resident training, inservice training, and an administrative structure geared directly toward training of residents (e.g., Risley & Favell, 1979; Watson, 1976). The positive benefits to residents and staff of providing for environmental enrichment (Horner, 1980) could also be presented and then implemented on a trial basis.

Another advantage of applying retrospective designs to the operation of facilities for the mentally retarded is that they provide another way to attain compliance with recent legislation regarding habilitation programs in these institutions, whereas present licensing surveys based on simply examining records clearly do not always do so (Repp & Barton, 1980). Monitoring of compliance should be as direct as possible, but as a first step beyond "paper compliance" retrospective designs may be useful. Prospective analyses have even more advantages of course, in that managers can make changes in current procedures as the data warrant.

As noted by Carr, Schnelle, and Kirchner (1980), conclusions based on retrospective studies must be made cautiously. In the present study not only was there no control over the timing and duration of treatments, but the treatments themselves were complex. Changes in management, for example, involved changes in both formal and informal policies and procedures, and changes in training were not simply training vs no training, but included complex training packages and various kinds of feedback to staff. Nevertheless, the results are consistent with those of previous studies demonstrating that feedback is necessary to get staff to implement programs for residents (Panyan et al., 1970; Patterson et al., 1976; Quilitch, 1975) and that withdrawal of supervision, as in the removal of the Agnews Training Team from the Program leads to less than optimal implementation of programs (Bassett & Blanchard, 1977; Montegar et al., 1977).

Another reason to be cautious in making conclusions on the basis of these data is that the dependent variables were not constructed and tested for validity and reliability but were used because they were already being collected. Therefore, there is a possibility that the two measures of restraint usage could have been reactively affected because of the emphasis by management and the Agnews Training Team on reducing them. There is, however, independent support for the validity of the dependent variables. During the normal work week, the authors were on the units on almost a daily basis and observed no incidents where restraint was used without being documented. Second, SIRs were mentioned by the Training Team much less frequently than restraint data, and data for SIRs were not used in the monthly memorandum to the units nor were reports of SIRs responded to in a contingent manner by the Agnews Training Team nor by the Program Director during the program's morning meetings. The fact that the data for SIRs covaried with the restraint data suggests that both were independent measures of the same phenomenon.

Although only weak inferences can be drawn from retrospective designs, they are important as sources of hypothese which later can be rigorously tested with planned experiments. Three hypotheses are generated by the present retrospective analysis. First, support by management of behavioral programming had large effects on the use of restraint in the Program. "Management support" could be defined operationally and its effects on efficiency in delivering services could be systematiclly tested. Some of the variables to be examined in this context could include number of expressions of support by program management at various levels of the organization, incorporation in an employee's annual review of questions regarding implementation of behavioral programs, etc.

A second hypothesis concerns the most efficient way to implement in a relatively unstructured program a "least restrictive environment" in which behavioral excesses are reduced while, at the same time, the restriction of human rights is minimized. The present study suggests that rather than trying to reduce each resident's behavior problems on an individual basis, it may be more efficient to introduce an interim step in which staff are trained to change the behavior of entire groups of residents. Once the groups are under control, individualized programs can be started more easily and with a greater chance for success.

Finally, in reducing behavior problems, Skinner (1978) has advocated the use of primarily positive methods. The present report highlights the extent to which this can be done, even under such less than optimal conditions as not having all staff trained, as having an annual staff turnover of approximately 50%, as not having a systematic attempt at environmental enrichment, and not giving systematic feedback to individual staff members for implementing programs. Although restraint and contingent observation were used when behaviors posed a danger to the resident himself or others, the focus of the training was primarily on reinforcing residents for various compliance behaviors. While no statements can be made regarding the effectiveness of using compliance training as a method of reducing behavior problems, the reductions in restraint usage are consistent with the recent report by Russo, Cataldo, and Cushing (1981) that such training can reduce the frequency of non-targeted behavior problems. Further research on such response covariation could have important implications for the use of behavioral techniques in large residential facilities because, as Russo et al. point out, it might be possible to reduce many serious behavior problems without applying restrictive procedures directly to them. Although this general approach would certainly not be effective or desirable in all cases, when used successfully it would be less restrictive and perhaps more cost effective than the intensive programs that are typically used with such behaviors.

REFERENCES

Bassett, J. E., & Blanchard, E. B. (1977). The effect of the absence of close supervision on the use of response cost in a prison token economy. *Journal of Applied Behavior Analysis, 10*, 375-379.

Bathazar, E. E. (1972). Residential programs in adaptive behavior for the emotionally disturbed more severely retarded. *Mental Retardation, 10*, 10-13.

Campbell, D. T., & Stanley, J. C. (1966). *Experimental and quasi-experimental designs for research*. Chicago: Rand McNally.

Carr, A. F., Schnelle, J. F., & Kirchner, R. E. (1980). Police crackdowns and slowdowns: A naturalistic evaluation of changes in police traffic enforcement. *Behavioral Assessment, 2*, 33-41.

Favell, J. E., Risley, T. R., Wolfe, A. F., Riddle, J. I., & Rasmussen, P. R. (1981). The limits of habilitation: How can we identify them and how can we change them? *Analysis and Intervention in Developmental Disabilities, 1*, 37-43.

Frederiksen, L. W., & Lovett, S. B. (1980). Inside organizational behavioral management: Perspectives on an emerging field. *Journal of Organizational Behavior Management, 2*, 193-203.

Gardner, J. M. (1972). Teaching behavior modification to nonprofessionals. *Journal of Applied Behavior Analysis, 5*, 517-521.

Hall, R. V., & Copeland, R. E. (1972). The responsive teaching model: A first step in shaping school personnel as behavior modification specialists. In F. W. Clark, D. R. Evans, & L. A. Hamerlynk (Eds.), *Implementing behavioral programs for schools and clinics*. Champaign, Illinois: Research Press.

Horner, R. D. (1980). The effects of an environmental "enrichment" program on the behavior of institutionalized profoundly retarded children. *Journal of Applied Behavior Analysis, 13*, 473-491.

Iwata, B. A., Bailey, J. S., Brown, K. M., Foshee, T. J., & Alpern, M. (1976). A performance-based lottery to improve residential care and training by institutional staff. *Journal of Applied Behavior Analysis, 9*, 417-431.

Klaber, M. M. (1969). The retarded and institutions for the retarded—a preliminary report. In S. Sarason & J. Doris (Eds.), *Psychological problems in mental deficiency*. New York: Harper & Row.

Lakin, K. C., Bruininks, R. H., Hill, B. K., & Hauber, F. A. (1982). Turnover of direct-care staff in a national sample of residential facilities of mentally retarded people. *American Journal of Mental Deficiency, 87*, 64-72.

Liberman, R. P. (1979). Comments on "Program Evaluation Research." *The Behavior Therapist, 2*, 8.

Martin, G. L. (1972). Teaching operant conditioning to psychiatric nurses, aids, and attendants. In F. W. Clark, D. R. Evans, & L. A. Hamerlynk (Eds.), *Implementing behavioral programs for schools and clinics*. Champaign, Illinois: Research Press.

Martin, R. (1975). *Legal challenges to behavior modification*. Champaign, Illinois: Research Press.

Montegar, C. A., Reid, D. H., Madsen, C. H., & Ewell, M. D. (1977). Increasing institutional staff to resident interactions through in-service training and supervisor approval. *Behavior Therapy, 8*, 533-540.

Panyan, M., Boozer, H., and Morris, N. (1979). Feedback to attendants as a reinforcer for applying operant techniques. *Journal of Applied Behavior Analysis, 3*, 1-4.

Patterson, E. T., Griffin, J. C., & Panyan, M. C. (1976). Incentive maintenance of self-help skill training programs for non-professional personnel. *Journal of Behavior Therapy and Experimental Psychiatry, 7*, 249-253.

Pommer, D. A., & Streedbeck, D. (1974). Motivating staff performance in an operant learning program for children. *Journal of Applied Behavior Analysis, 7*, 217-221.

Pomerleau, O. F., Bobrove, P. H., & Smith, R. H. (1973). Rewarding psychiatric aides for the behavior improvement of assigned patients. *Journal of Applied Behavior Analysis, 6*, 383-390.

Porterfield, J. K., Herbert-Jackson, E., & Risley, T. R. (1976). Contingent observation: An effective and acceptable procedure for reducing disruptive behavior of young children in a group setting. *Journal of Applied Behavior Analysis, 9*, 55-64.

Quilitch, H. R. (1975). A comparison of three staff-management procedures. *Journal of Applied Behavior Analysis, 8*, 59-66.

Repp, A. C., & Barton, L. E. (1980). Naturalistic observations of institutionalized retarded persons: A comparison of licensure decisions and behavioral observations. *Journal of Applied Behavior Analysis, 13*, 333-341.

Risley, T. R., & Favell, J. (1979). Constructing a living environment in an institution. In L. A. Hamerlynk (Ed.), *Behavioral systems for the developmentally disabled: II. Institutional, clinic, and community environments.* New York: Brunner/Mazel.

Russo, D. C., Cataldo, M. F., & Cushing, P. J. (1981). Compliance training and behavioral covariation in the treatment of multiple behavior problems. *Journal of Applied Behavior Analysis, 14*, 209-222.

Skinner, B. F. *Reflections on behaviorism and society.* Englewood Cliffs, N.J.: Prentice Hall, 1978.

Watson, L. S. (1976). Shaping and maintaining behavior modification skills in staff using contingent reinforcement techniques. In R. L. Patterson (Ed.), *Maintaining effective token economies.* Springfield, Illinois: Charles C. Thomas.

Welsch, W. V., Ludwig, C., Radiker, J. E., & Krapfl, J. E. (1973). Effects of feedback on daily completion of behavior modification projects. *Mental Retardation, 10*, 24-26.

Ziarnik, J. P., & Bernstein, G. S. (1982). A critical examination of the effect of inservice training on staff performance. *Mental Retardation, 20*, 109-114.

A Case Study Examining the Effectiveness and Cost of Incentive Programs to Reduce Staff Absenteeism in a Preschool

Jinger Robins
Margaret Lloyd

ABSTRACT. Most employers provide some number of paid sick leave days for their employees. If employees use their sick leave days by calling in sick on days they are feeling well, productivity (in terms of either goods or services) may be reduced. In this study, conducted at a preschool, productivity was defined as the number of children enrolled each month. In baseline, the 13 full-time employees were absent 4% of the time and 75 children were enrolled. The effectiveness and cost of two voluntary incentive programs designed to reduce employee absenteeism were examined for 4-½ years in a single case experimental design. The absenteeism of employees who volunteered to participate in the incentive program was .7% and overall absenteeism during the incentive programs was 2-½% while costs remained constant. Twenty-six percent more children were served. Employees preferred monetary to non-monetary incentives.

Private and public sector employers are concerned about employee withdrawal because of its potential impact on the production of goods or services. Employee withdrawal includes behaviors such as tardiness, poor performance, absenteeism, and quitting. Most of the literature related to withdrawal focuses on absenteeism and quitting. These behaviors are the easiest to measure and probably the most costly (Zaharia and Baumeister, 1978). While the

This paper was based on a thesis submitted by the first author to the Graduate School of Drake University in partial fulfillment of the requirement of the MA degree. Reprints may be obtained from Margaret Lloyd, Department of Psychology, Drake University, Des Moines, IA 50311.

175

primary cause of absenteeism was formerly thought to be lack of job satisfaction, recent reviews of the literature have found that relationship to be a weak one, implying that other variables must be involved (Steers and Rhodes, 1978). These variables fall into three broad categories; extra-institutional variables, e.g., inflation rates; intra-institutional variables, e.g., sick leave policies; and variables which are idiosyncratic to a particular employee, e.g., distance the employee must travel to get to work (Zaharia and Baumeister, 1978). Stated more behaviorally, some aspect of the working environment might cause illnesses and excessive absenteeism, as it might for example, in an asbestos factory; otherwise, the balance of the consequences of illegitimate absenteeism (absenteeism without illness) must be more reinforcing than the balance of the consequences for attending work. For example, an employee might find that the reinforcers of playing golf and avoiding an irritable supervisor while receiving sick-leave pay outweigh the reinforcers associated with going to work.

Employers cannot control those reinforcers for absenteeism that would be categorized as extra-institutional or idiosyncratic. Oftentimes elimination of positive and negative intra-institutional reinforcers for absenteeism is difficult. For this reason, a number of contingency arrangements have been designed to override the reinforcers for excessive absenteeism. Successful incentive systems for attendance have been based on monetary rewards (Nord, 1970; Hermann, de Montes, Dominquez, Montes, and Hopkins, 1973; Orpen, 1978) and such non-monetary incentives as freedom from the requirement to punch the time clock, approved time off without pay and a reduction in position on the disciplinary ladder (Kempen & Hall, 1977). Lottery systems based on monetary (Nord, 1970; Pedalino and Gamboa, 1974; Wallin & Johnson, 1976) and non-monetary prizes, e.g., lunch with the unit supervisor, re-arrangement of days off, and days without lunchroom duty or client training sessions, (Shoemaker & Reid, 1980) have also been demonstrated to be effective. Evidence suggests that incentive programs developed jointly by employees and employers may be more effective, for longer periods of time, than programs which are simply imposed on employees by management (Scheflen, Lawler & Hackman, 1971).

The incentive programs are consistent with the behavioral perspective which considers behaviors as problems to be managed rather than symptoms of underlying causes. No symptom substitution has been reported when absenteeism has been reduced by these direct control procedures. To the extent intra-institutional factors that encourage absenteeism can be reduced, direct control procedures can help decrease absenteeism even more (Kempen, 1982). Extra-institutional and idiosyncratic causes of absenteeism will not be removed in the near future.

BACKGROUND

The organizational setting for this intervention was a preschool serving approximately 75 children from low income families of several ethnic backgrounds. Absenteeism at the preschool was about 4%, less than the 6.5% usually reported for direct care personnel (Zaharia and Baumeister, 1978) but nevertheless a serious problem for this particular facility. The amount of Title 20 federal funding for the preschool's daily operation was based upon the number of children enrolled, but the preschool was only eligible for the funding if specific employee-child ratios were met. The number of employees required to be present varied on a daily basis according to the number of children, in each of several age ranges, who were in attendance. One staff member was required to be present for each four children who were 2 years old, each six children who were 3 years old, each seven children who were 4 years old and each eight children who were 5 or 6 years old. Although the preschool had a waiting list of 10-15 names at any given time, these children could not be enrolled because of the ratio requirements. Unannounced spot checks were made by federal and state employees to see if the required ratios were being met. The preschool administration had been informed that the prescribed ratios were not being met and that continued federal funding and state licensing of the preschool were in jeopardy. The preschool did not have the funds to pay for substitute employees when permanent employees were absent on sick leave.

Several intra-institutional factors may have contributed to absenteeism. Throughout the 4-½ years of this study, employee salaries ranged from $3,100 to 11,800 per year depending upon the employee's education and experience. Certified teachers at the top of the preschool's salary scale often made $3,000 less per year than certified teachers in the public school system. Employees may have felt justified in taking sick leave when they were not really sick since their salaries were so low.

Difficult working conditions may also have been a factor. The preschool was housed in an old church. Dividers such as desks and children's lockers were used to separate the age groups from one another resulting in a noise problem. The building was not airconditioned and temperatures in the summer often reached 100° F. In the winter, the heating system which was controlled by the landlord, was not properly regulated. Employees may have found working conditions so aversive that they preferred staying home.

A third factor may have been the "pooling process." Groups at the preschool consisted of 15 to 30 children, one head teacher, one assistant teacher and one or more aides, depending on ratio requirements. If a staff absence occurred in a group, another employee was pulled from his or her job to maintain the required teacher-child ratio, e.g., if the nurse had to take over an aide position, then other employees had to do first aide duties as well as their own jobs. The absence of any employee resulted in more work for the remaining employees and often put the remaining employees in the position of having to do tasks which were not part of their job descriptions.

A fourth factor may have been the health of the children and, consequently, of the employees. Contagious illness and parasites were often present at the preschool, e.g., body lice, head lice, ringworm, chicken pox, and measles. Employees often came into contact with infected children before the nurse had an opportunity to conduct the daily inspection. Employees may have been sick more often than they would have been had they been working in another environment.

In addition to these factors, the preschool sick leave policy encouraged employees to stay home, at least occasionally, when they were not actually sick. Employees had 15 paid sick leave days per year and therefore might take several days off for reasons other than illness and still have enough paid days left to cover ordinary illness. Also, employees were not allowed to accumulate more than 30 days sick leave. Those who had done so either had to use or lose the sick leave days they accumulated in excess of this limit. Finally, a similar situation existed for employees who quit, since they did not get any financial remuneration for the sick leave days they had accumulated.

The preschool administrator was unable to manipulate the first four factors suspected of contributing to absenteeism and therefore their effects could not be either measured or reduced directly. The preschool's remaining option was to override their effects by altering the sick leave policy. Since the literature suggests that incentive programs have reduced absenteeism in other settings, incentives for attendance were incorporated into the preschool sick leave policy. The preschool had two goals in relation to the absenteeism problem. One was to reduce overall rates of absenteeism; the second was to regulate absenteeism so that several employees were not absent at the same time. The experimenters had two additional goals: to examine the cost and effectiveness of voluntary incentive programs designed to reduce absenteeism and to discover the kinds of incentives chosen by employees when several were concurrently available.

METHOD

Subjects

All full-time employees of a preschool located in a mid-western city participated in this study. Part-time and Central Iowa Employment Training Consortium (CETA) employees were excluded since they were not covered by preschool sick leave policies. Positions held by full time employees consisted of head teacher, social worker, aide, and assistant cook. Employees came and went during the 55 months of the study. As an example of employee characteristics, during the last three months of baseline, eight women and one man were employed full-time. Median age was 36; the youngest employed was 22, the oldest 72. One employee had completed grammar school; seven, high school; and one had had two years at a bible college. Five employees were the sole support of their families. Average length of employment was three years and three months.

Dependent Measures

An absence was recorded if an employee was not at the preschool for four or more consecutive hours of an eight hour work day. The number of absences for each employee was recorded from daily sign-in sheets. Employees signed in when they arrived at work in the morning. Paychecks were based on sign-in sheets. If an employee left at some time during the day, the head teacher for his or her group noted this on the sign-in sheet and initiated the "pooling" process. It was thus extremely unlikely that an absence would remain unnoticed. Percent absenteeism was calculated by dividing the number of absences by the total number of scheduled work days. Employees' annual salaries were recorded from payroll records. Data from all records were reviewed by two investigators. Inter-reliability in transferring data from these sources was 100%.

Baseline Sick Leave Contingencies

The preschool's established absentee policy was in effect from March, 1977, through August, 1979. Each employee automatically accumulated 1.25 sick leave days in his or her sick leave account each month. If an employee was absent for a day (and had at least one day accumulated in his or her account) the employee was paid for that day and one day was deducted from the total in the account. Employees were not paid when they were absent if they did not have any days in their accounts. No more than 30 sick leave days could be accumulated at any time during an employee's total length of employment. Other leave consisted of 3.33 days per year for funeral leave and 5 to 20 days per year for vacation depending upon length of service. Baseline contingencies were in effect for 28 months of data collection prior to the incentive programs and for three months afterwards.

Bonus Program

Employees were eligible to join the bonus program if they had accumulated at least five days in their sick leave accounts. The five day minimum was established to safeguard employees against actual illness. Employees who were eligible to join the bonus program and wished to do so were required to submit a written request. Participating employees who had no absences for a full calendar month received $20.00 bonuses instead of accumulating 1.25 sick leave days in their sick leave accounts. (The mean cost to the preschool of 1.25 days of paid sick leave was $21.00.) A participating employee who was absent during the month did not receive $20.00; instead, 1.25 sick leave days were added to his/her account and the number of days the employee was absent was subtracted. Initially, employees were to be allowed to join or leave the bonus program every month. After one month, this was changed to every three months in order to reduce bookkeeping problems. The bonus program was in effect for 13 months.

Choice Program

Several incentives were made available from which eligible employees (i.e., employees who had five days in their sick leave accounts), who requested to participate, could choose. Employees decided upon the various incentives in conjunction with the preschool administration. A different choice could be made at the beginning of each 3-month period. An employee could choose to:

1. receive a $20.00 bonus following a month without an absence,
2. take one extra day-off scheduled so as not to upset employee/child ratios following a month without an absence,
3. receive a $75.00 bonus following three months without an absence,
4. take three extra consecutive days-off scheduled so as not to upset employee/child ratios following three months without an absence,
5. choose one of three alternatives to follow each month without an absence. The alternatives were: a T-shirt with the name and address of the preschool on it; lunch at a restaurant with the director of the preschool at the preschool's expense; and two free bottles of soda a day for the next month.

Any participating employee who was absent during a month did not receive the selected incentive but accumulated and lost sick leave days in the standard way provided for by the pre-school policy. Employees had the opportunity to join or leave the choice program once every three months. The program was in effect for nine months.

In summary, absenteeism was monitored during 28 months while the preschool's standard sick leave policy was in effect, then for 15 months of the bonus program, 9 months of the choice program and finally for 3 more months of the standard sick leave policy.

RESULTS

The percent of work-days employees were absent during 3 month blocks was calculated by dividing the number of absences by the number of scheduled working days. Figure 1 shows that in baseline preschool absenteeism was running about 4%.

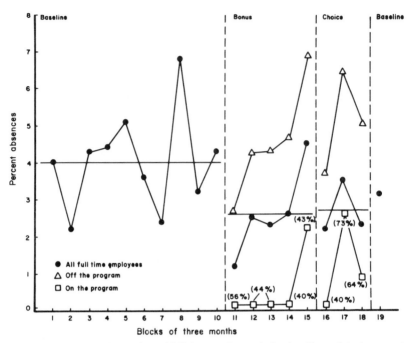

FIGURE 1. Percent absenteeism of full time employees during baseline and the bonus and choice of incentives programs. The percent of employees enrolled in a given program is indicated in parentheses. All blocks, except block 11, span 3 calendar months. Block 11 represents 1 month.

When the bonus program was made available, only four employees were eligible for it and all chose to go on the program. Several employees became eligible for and went on the program later; some became eligible but did not choose to go on the program; two employees went on, then off, then back on the program at different times. Overall preschool absenteeism, i.e., absenteeism for all full-time employees, decreased from 4% to about 2.6%, during the bonus program. The percent of absences for employees on the bonus program was 0% for four consecutive blocks and then increased to 2.2% in block 15 while the percent of absences for employees who either chose not to go on the program or were ineligible for it steadily increased from 2.6% in the 11th block to 6.7% in the 15th block.

The change from the bonus to choice conditions was timed unfortunately. The plans for the choice program were devised during the last half of block 15. The data available at the time (blocks 11-14) were very stable. By the time it became apparent that absenteeism had increased during block 15, the planning for the choice program was too far advanced, in the estimation of the preschool administration, to be rescinded.

During the nine months the choice program was available, overall preschool absenteeism remained essentially unchanged at 2.6%. The percent of absences for employees who were in the choice program was 0, 2.6% and .9% in blocks 16, 17, and 18 respectively. The percent of absences for employees who were not eligible for the program or chose not to go on the program was 3.6%, 6.4% and 5%. These functions were essentially parallel with a difference of about 4% in favor of employees who chose to go on the program.

When all employees were once again under the original preschool absentee policy, absenteeism increased to 3.1%. No statistical analyses were performed on the data because of the violation of assumptions, for example the number of employees changed from month to month, employees went in and out of experimental conditions at will and so forth.

Figure 2 permits analysis of the costs of the incentive programs and the baseline absentee policy. The upper portion of Figure 2 shows the average annual salary of employees working in each three month block. The average annual salary steadily increased from $5,300 to $9,400 over the 55 months of this study. This increase reflected both inflation and the fact that three certified teachers were hired during block 15 while no certified teacher had been on staff prior to that time. Certified teachers were the most highly paid employees; they were paid more than head teachers who were not certified. However, it should be mentioned that low rates of absenteeism were not a result of hiring higher paid employees. During blocks 15 and 16, before any of the three teachers volunteered for the incentive program, the combined absenteeism was 5.5%.

The middle portion of Figure 2 shows the mean cost of absenteeism per employee during three month periods. This was calculated in baseline by multiplying the mean daily salary by the mean number of paid sick leave days taken each three months. During the incentive programs, it was calculated by multiplying the mean daily salary by the mean number of paid sick leave days and adding in the mean cost of incentives. The cost of absenteeism per employee increased from $54 in block 1 to $92 in block 17.

The bottom portion of Figure 2 shows the mean cost of absen-

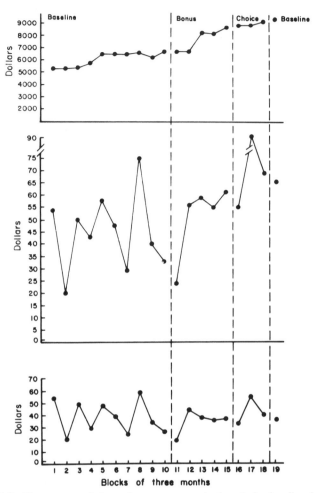

FIGURE 2. The upper panel shows the average annual salary during baseline, bonus program and choice of incentives programs. The middle panel shows the mean cost of sick leave paid to each employee during baseline and the mean actual cost of sick leave plus the cost of incentives during bonus and choice incentives programs. The lower panel shows those costs corrected for inflation and disproportionate hiring of high salaried employees. All blocks except block 11, span 3 calendar months.

teeism per employee corrected for inflation and the disproportionate hiring of high salaried employees. This was calculated by first dividing $5300, the average annual salary in block 1, by the average annual salary in each succeeding three month block. For example, the average salary in block 1 was 59% of the average salary in block 16. The mean cost of absenteeism for each block was then multiplied by this percentage. For example, the mean cost of absenteeism in block 16, $55, was multiplied by 59%. The resulting figure, $32, is comparable to the mean cost of absenteeism in block 1 which was $54, i.e., it represents the cost of absenteeism in block 16 adjusted for inflation and the hiring of more highly salaried employees. Corrected costs were fairly stable across all conditions with a slight increase during the bonus and choice programs. The mean across all blocks was $41.

Figure 3 permits an analysis of productivity at the preschool.

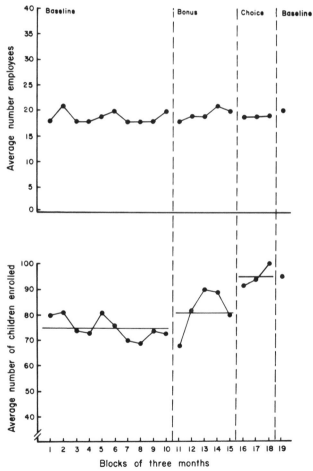

FIGURE 3. The upper panel shows the average number of employees on payroll. The bottom panel shows the mean daily enrollment of children. All blocks, except block 11, span 3 calendar months. Block 11 represents 1 calendar month.

Productivity was defined as the number of children who could be served while maintaining acceptable employee-child ratios. The top portion of Figure 3 shows the number of employees on payroll for each 3 month block including part-time and CETA employees. The average number of employees on payroll was fairly stable across all conditions, ranging from 18 to 21. Approximately six part-time and CETA employees and approximately 13 full-time employees were on payroll each block. The bottom portion of Figure 3 shows the mean daily enrollment of children for each 3 month block. Daily enrollment showed a slightly decreasing trend through baseline; the mean enrollment was 75. Daily enrollment increased with the introduction of both bonus pay and choice programs. Approximately 82 children were served each day during the bonus pay program and approximately 95 in the choice program. Figures 2 and 3 together show that while the cost of absenteeism remained constant across baseline and the incentive program, productivity increased 26%.

Table 1 shows the alternatives chosen by employees in the choice of incentives program. Twenty-two (out of 27) choices were for

Table 1

The Number of Employees Choosing Each Alternative During the Choice of Incentives Program for each Three Month Block

Option	Block 16	Block 17	Block 18
$20 payment	1	5	5
One day off after one month			2
$75 after three months	6	4	1
Three days off after three months		1	1
Choice of three alternatives		1	

bonuses. Half (11) of those choices were for the higher-risk, higher payoff bonus, $75, which required 3 months of perfect attendance. However, a clear shift in preference from high risk and high payoff incentives to incentives with less risk and less payoff ($20 each month) occurred across blocks, i.e., 1 employee opted for the low risk bonus and 6 employees opted for the high risk bonus in block 16, while 5 employees opted for the low risk bonus and 1 opted for high risk bonus in block 18. The last month of block 16 was December; employees may have been saving up to pay for Christmas presents.

DISCUSSION

The situation vis a vis absenteeism in this preschool may have been somewhat unique in two respects. First, absenteeism, even in baseline, was not inordinately high. However, given the double bind funding situation, i.e., funding depended on low teacher-child ratios but was inadequate to maintain those ratios, even 4% absenteeism threatened the continuance of the preschool program. Second, it was not important that the incentive programs affect every employee equally. They only had to affect some employees enough that overall absenteeism would drop below baseline levels. The latter made the voluntary element of the incentive program possible.

It is worth noting that employees not only had the option of volunteering, but also had to earn the right to participate. It is possible that the absence of forced participation contributed to the surprisingly low levels of overall absenteeism (2-½%) seen during the incentive programs. The effectiveness of the bonus and choice of incentives programs in reducing absenteeism was not fully verified experimentally in this study because of the brief, 3 month return to baseline. However, that briefness provided a social validation of the effectiveness of the incentive programs. The preschool administration refused to remain in baseline any longer than 3 months. They judged they were already observing an increase in absenteeism which could potentially lead to a decrease in the average number of children who could be enrolled and the potential consequence of a reduction in Title 20 funding. The bonus program was re-established after block 19. The choice program was not used because of difficulty in scheduling days-off so they would not affect employee-child ratios and because employees rarely chose anything other than monetary incentives even when the opportunity to do so was available. The experimenters withdrew from the situation at this point.

Several facts suggest that the bonus and choice programs were responsible for the observed reduction in employee absenteeism: (1) overall absenteeism decreased when the incentive programs were available, and (2) employees who were on the incentive program consistently showed less absenteeism than employees who were not.

The latter finding might have been expected since participating employees were self selected. This is, perhaps, the baseline absenteeism of employees who chose to go on the program was less than that of employees who chose not to. This was certainly true during the first two treatment data points (4 months). The four employees who chose to go on the bonus program had low levels of absenteeism in baseline (approximately 1.5%). However, the bonus program reduced their absenteeism enough (0%) to substantially affect *overall* absenteeism rates at the preschool, i.e., the program did more than just separate the data of the employees who tended to be absent a lot from the data of the employees who did not. (After the first two blocks, the addition and removal of employees from the program made this kind of analysis meaningless—i.e., almost every employee had been on the program at some time.)

A factor which would have worked against the observation of both (1) and (2) above was that employees, especially newly hired employees, had to hold their absences down in order to accumulate the five sick leave days required for program eligibility. To this extent, then, the incentive programs could reduce absenteeism of employees who were not yet on the program.

Prior to the implementation of the incentive programs, records were not kept of the number of times, if any, that an employee was sent home from work by the nurse because of an actual illness. Records kept during the incentive programs indicated that an employee was sent home by the nurse on only two occasions. Apparently, the incentive programs did not create conditions which encouraged many employees to come to work when they were actually ill.

The choice program was devised for this study because it was thought that offering employees a number of incentives from which to choose would be analogous to having a reinforcer menu or a token store. Employees could choose the incentive (e.g., $20, soda, a day off) most appropriate to their current deprivation. The choice program did not reduce absenteeism in this particular setting any further than the bonus program. Since most employees chose monetary incentives in the choice program, providing a range of nonmonetary incentives appears to have been an irrelevance. The use of monetary incentives for attendance did not result in increased costs for the preschool. Costs remained constant throughout all conditions. However, during baseline, payments were made to employees for calling in sick, while during the incentive programs, payments were made for perfect attendance. This shift in contingencies apparently led to a decrease in absenteeism, an improvement in teacher-child ratios, the renewal of the state license and continued Title 20 funding.

REFERENCES

Hermann, J. A., de Montes, A. I., Dominquez, B., Montes, F., & Hopkins, B. L. (1973). Effects of bonuses for punctuality on the tardiness of industrial workers. *Journal of Applied Behavior Analysis, 6*, 563-570.

Kempen, R. W. (1982). Absenteeism and tardiness. In L. W. Frederiksen (Ed), *Handbook of Organizational Behavior Management*. New York: Wiley.

Kempen, R. W., & Hall, V. R. (1977). Reduction of industrial absenteeism: Results of a behavioral approach. *Journal of Organizational Behavior Management, 1*, 1-21.

Nord, W. (1970). Improving attendance through rewards. *Personnel Administration*, 37-41.

Orpen, C. (1978). Effects of bonuses for attendance on the absenteeism of industrial workers. *Journal of Organizational Behavior Management, 1*, 118-124.

Pedalino, E., & Gamboa, V. U. (1974). Behavior modification and absenteeism: Intervention in one industrial setting. *Journal of Applied Psychology, 59*, 694-698.

Shoemaker, J., & Reid, D. H. (1980). Decreasing chronic absenteeism among institutional staff: Effects of a low-cost attendance program. *Journal of Organizational Behavior Management, 2*, 317-328.

Silva, D. B., Duncan, P. K. & Doudna, D. (1981). The effects of attendance-contingent feedback and praise on attendance a work efficiency. *Journal of Organizational Behavior Management, 3*, 59-69.

Wallin, J. A., & Johnson, R. D. (1976). The positive reinforcement approach to controlling employee absenteeism. *Personnel Journal*, August, 390-392.

Scheflen, K. C., Lawler, E. E., & Hackmann, J. R. (1971). Long-term impact of employee participation in the development of pay incentive plans: a field experiment revisited. *Journal of Applied Psychology, 55*, 182-186.

Steers, R., & Rhodes, S. (1978). Major influences on employee attendance: A process model. *Journal of Applied Psychology, 63*, 391-407.

Zaharia, E. S., & Baumeister, A. A. (1978). Technician turnover and absenteeism in public residential facilities. *American Journal of Mental Deficiency, 82*, 580-593.

GUEST REVIEWERS—VOLUME 5

Kenneth N. Anchor
Behavior Management
Consultants, Inc.

Ted D. Apking
Kelly Services, Inc.

James Austin
Virginia Polytechnic Institute
and State University

Walter Christian
May Institute

Robert Collins
Behavior Management
Consultants, Inc.

David Dean
Kepner-Tregor, Incorporated

Phillip K. Duncan
West Chester University

Daniel Fishman
Rutgers University

E. Scott Geller
Virginia Polytechnic Institute
and State University

Robert Haynes
Performance Technologies
Corporation

Carl Merle Johnson
Central Michigan University

Richard P. Johnson
Northeast Community Mental
Health Center

Abby C. King
Stanford University

Timothy Koltuniak
Veterans Administration
Hospital
Montrose, New York

Steve Lovett
Veterans Administration
Hospital
Palo Alto, California

Terry McSween
Performance Systems
Improvement

Sheldon Pinsky
Iowa State University

Gregory C. Murphy
Preston Institute
of Technology

Andrew G. Remenyi
Lincoln Institute of Health
Services

Paul C. Ross
American Telephone
and Telegraph Company

James Rudd
Virginia Polytechnic Institute
and State University

John F. Schnelle
Middle Tennessee State
University

Paul H. Selden
Performance Management,
Inc.

Laura S. Solomon
University of Vermont

Beth Sulzer-Azaroff
University of Connecticut

Halina Wurzelman
Veterans Administration
Hospital
Brockton, Massachusetts

Jack Zigon
Yellow Freight System, Inc.

AUTHOR INDEX TO VOLUME 5[1]

---

[1]This is a comprehensive index of authors contributing to Volume 5 of the *Journal of Organizational Behavior Management*. The present volume, *Improving Staff Effectiveness in Human Service Settings* was also published as the third and fourth issue of this volume. Issues Number 1 and 2 have been published as separate issues of the *Journal*.